Revive Your Mainline Congregation

Revive your mainline congregation

Prescriptions for **Vital Church Life**

Robert D. Schieler

The Pilgrim Press
Cleveland

This book is dedicated to

Our Lord Jesus Christ, who is the Sole Head of the Church; my wife Charmaine, for her love, participation, support, and encouragement in my ministries of forty-three plus years; Lyle Campbell, Dean Spencer, and John Pruehs for their help and support in initiating and developing the Church Vitality Center and recommending, even insisting, that I write this book!

The Pilgrim Press, 700 Prospect Avenue East, Cleveland, Ohio 44115-11000
pilgrimpress.com
© 2003 Robert D. Schieler

All rights reserved. Published 2003
Printed in the United States of America on acid-free paper
08 07 06 05 04 03   5 4 3 2 1

Library of Congress Cataloging-in-Publication Data

Schieler, Robert D., 1934–
    Revive your mainline congregation : prescriptions for vital church life /
Robert D. Schieler.
      p.   cm.
    Includes bibliographical references.
    ISBN 0-8298-1581-3 (pbk. : alk. paper)
    1. Church renewal—United States.   2. Protestant churches—United States
  I. Title.

BV600.3.S35   2003
250'.973—dc22

                                                                    2003066367

Contents

chapter one

The Characteristics of Living versus Dying Churches

MAINLINE PROTESTANT CHURCHES can live again! They don't have to die! They can become vital centers of Christian life and mission as they once were! But to succeed, they must be *willing to change* and *do most things differently* than they have been doing in the last thirty-five to fifty years.

empty tomb, inc., a Christian research group based in Champaign-Urbana, IL,[1] has graphed the severe declines in mainline Protestant churches since the 1960s. On the basis of straight line projections, the figures reveal that unless mainline Protestant churches do things significantly differently than over the past thirty-five to fifty years, most United Church of Christ congregations (my denomination, for example) will be gone by 2032—and that is just thirty years away—following a steady decline since 1965. The United Church of Christ has lost more than 700,000 members and more than 1,000 churches in that brief amount of time, and the decline has shown no signs of turning around. Moreover, the "empty tomb, inc." figures reveal that the rest of the mainline churches will have similar fates within a few years thereafter!

Why are mainline churches is such dire straits? When I work with churches, I ask, "If the business or corporation for which you work today, or your farms, were organized, operated, and, for the most part, doing the same things in the same ways they were a half century ago, what would happen to your business, corporation, or farm?" Without hesitation they respond, "They would be gone!"

Then I ask, "Is your church organized, operated, and, for the most part, doing most of the same things in the same ways they were thirty-five to fifty years ago? When you worship today, do you sing essentially the same hymns and responses (the Gloria Patri, Doxology, etc.)? Do you hear the same Calls to Worship, Invocations, Confessions of Sin, Assurances of Pardon, and so on? Do you hear the same choir anthems, as well as sermons that sound strangely familiar? Do you have most or all of the same committees, boards, and organizations? Do you schedule many of the same activities that you had thirty-five to fifty years ago?" And, again, without hesitating, they respond with a loud "Yes!"

Then I ask, "And what is happening to your church?" In most cases I hear, "Our church has been losing members for years; worship attendance is half or less than half of what it used to be; our choir keeps getting smaller (or we don't have a choir anymore); we have very few children or youth, not really enough to have a Sunday school or youth group; we have constant financial problems, so much so that we had to reduce our staff to the bare minimum; we are having difficulty keeping up the maintenance on our aging building; we have trouble finding enough volunteers to fill our committees, and those few committees we have left have poor attendance; we can't find enough Sunday school teachers; and people don't attend church social events as they once did."

Then I ask the final question, "What is your church's vision for the future; what is your church going to be like five to ten years from now?" Too often I hear, "Our church will be gone," which is usually accompanied by tears. My response is, "If that is your vision of your church's future, then you are already working both consciously and subconsciously to bring it about, and you will undoubtedly succeed! Your church will die! But, if you formulate a new vision, a vision of what God and Jesus want this church to be five to ten years from now, then you will seek it both consciously and subconsciously, and with God leading, guiding, and empowering you, you will probably achieve it."

So mainline churches don't have to die! They can become "alive" again, if they are willing to be the church of Jesus Christ seeking to transform the present and the future, rather than perpetuating the past, if they are willing to change and do most things differently than they have for the past thirty-five to fifty years.

This book will delineate some of the distinguishing characteristics, the marks of living churches versus dying churches, as I have experienced and witnessed within mainline Protestant churches over the past forty-plus years of ministry as a pastor, judicatory staff person, and consultant with churches for the past ten years. It will reveal not only what needs to be done to turn churches around, but also how mainline churches that are surviving and thriving in this new age are "doing it."

This is not to say that all churches must do the same things in the same ways, for each church is somewhat unique. Yet, there are certain basic biblical-theological understandings of the nature and mission of the church that many mainline churches have been ignoring—or outright rebelling against. There are ways to reorganize churches that will help them become vital outposts of Christ's ministries once again, as well as to change organizational patterns that hinder and stop churches from accomplishing Christ's mission in the world today. Moreover, there are strategies and methods that are working and not working in our new world today for doing significant ministry and mission. This book will attempt to share both what is working and not working today in mainline Protestantism.

Here then are the characteristics of living versus dying churches as I have experienced and witnessed them. Each of these will be expanded upon with greater detail in the ensuing pages. The reader will note that more space has been devoted to the ministries of evangelism, worship, and stewardship than the others. This is because I believe that these are the three most neglected ministries within mainline churches today, therefore needing more attention and more change—although significant change is called for in all the ministries.

The Characteristics of Living versus Dying Churches

LIVING CHURCHES	DYING CHURCHES

AUTHORITY

1. *Jesus is the basic authority as "the sole head of the church."*	The congregation, council, trustees, pastor, or a layperson is the basic authority!

VISION

2. *There is a God-given vision of the church's future.*	There is no vision of where the church is going.

MISSION

3. *A clear, concise mission statement exists, along with specific, concrete strategies to achieve that mission and vision.*	No clear, concise mission statement exists, nor any specific, concrete strategies to achieve a mission and vision.

CHURCH ORGANIZATION

4. *Church organization is based on a biblical model.*	Church organization is based on a human/democratic model.
5. *The church is organized according to ministries (worship/spiritual growth, evangelism, congregational care, Christian education, youth, wider mission, buildings and grounds, stewardship, and Christian witness in society.*	The church is organized according to committees/boards (deacons, elders, trustees, worship, music, ushers, greeters, finance, fellowship, Christian education, memorials, etc.).

6. *All able members are expected and encouraged to participate in one ministry of the church every year.*

A few members are elected to committees/boards with two- to three-year terms. Thus, a small group provides leadership for the church.

7. *All members are led through a spiritual gifts inventory by a Spiritual Gifts Ministry team to help them discern their God-given spiritual gifts, and members are "commanded" by God to use them in a related ministry.*

Selected persons are recruited by a nominating committee, who too often seek people "who are breathing and who will say yes."

8. *Persons with spiritual gifts for certain ministries may continue to work in those ministries for as long as they have the gifts, sense a "calling" from God, and have passion for them.*

Members of committees are elected for a prescribed time (usually two to three years) after which they must stop and be elected to another committee for which they may or may not be gifted; or if they are not elected again, they may have to stop serving altogether.

9. *Ministry teams gather to "do ministry" (plan/rehearse for worship; lead Bible studies, train people to evangelize; visit the unchurched, sick and homebound; teach children, youth, and adults; aid the homeless, build homes, feed the hungry, etc.).*

Committee/board members meet primarily to "set policy," then go home and forget about it until next month when they gather to approve minutes, hear reports, and set more policy.

10. *People who "do ministry" for which they are "gifted" tend to find satisfaction, excitement, genuine involvement, and fulfillment.*	Committee/board members tend to "burn out," become bored, feel they are "going through motions," and "wasting their valuable time"—and attendance lags.
11. *Persons engaged in "ministry" are participating as "servants," obeying the call of God, who commands them to use their spiritual gifts in correlating ministries.*	Committee/board members see themselves as "volunteers" (they choose to do this, or at least allow themselves to be elected).

ROLES OF PASTOR(S)/STAFF

12. *The role of pastor(s) is to "equip the saints" for ministry to enable all members to do ministry.*	The pastor(s)/staff are paid to do the ministries of the church while the laity "set policy" and perform more "secular" tasks.
13. *The church seeks to build the staff as quickly as possible to keep providing more ministries for more people.*	The church seeks to keep the staff at a bare minimum to keep costs down.

EXPECTATIONS

14. *High expectations lead to high results!*	Low expectations lead to low results!

EVANGELISM

15. *Evangelism is considered the primary mission of the church!*	Evangelism has been almost completely neglected for the last fifty years, or at best is low on the priority scale.

16. *Evangelism is engaged in to enable all to live under the reign of God on earth for their own well-being and that of the whole world.*

New members are sought to help pay the bills and to staff the church's committee.

17. *All members of the church are expected and trained to participate in the ministry of evangelism.*

Evangelism is the work of the pastor and evangelism committee (if there is one).

18. *Each ministry of the church develops an evangelistic thrust.*

All committees of the church are separate and each does its own work.

WORSHIP

19. *Worship is designed to reach the unchurched (never been to church) and the dechurched (once active, no longer), as well as the current members. Thus, both traditional and contemporary worship services are offered.*

Worship is designed to connect with the current members; only traditional worship is offered.

20. *Worship uses the language, music, and technology of the people it is trying to reach (the 50 to 60 percent unchurched/ dechurched of our time), as well as that of the current members.*

Worship uses solely the language, music, and technology of the current members (mainly those over fifty-five years old).

21. *Worship is Holy Spirit–filled!*

Worship is often Holy Spirit–less, mainly going through motions, forms, and rituals.

22. *Worship is planned by a worship team (pastor and music, drama, and visuals directors).*

Worship is planned by the pastor with musical offerings supplied by the music staff.

23. *Worship planning for contemporary services begins with contemporary life situations, then reaches back to the Bible for guidance and answers. Planning for traditional services begins with prescribed lectionary verses and seeks to make them relevant.*

Worship planning begins with prescribed lectionary Bible verses, then attempts to make them meaningful.

STEWARDSHIP

24. *In stewardship, the mission is to develop faithful stewards of God's overwhelming, unfailing abundance.*

The mission is to raise enough money to pay the bills, preferably from nonmembers via fund raisers.

25. *A comprehensive, year-round ministry of stewardship is developed that includes stewardship education of the congregation, annual stewardship growth events (campaigns), a spiritual gift ministry to help all to discern their spiritual gifts and to*

A periodic committee raises the necessary monies for the next year.

participate in one ministry each year, and a continuing ministry gifts program (church endowment fund).

26. *All members are expected, encouraged, and helped to become tithers or tithers-in-process as a "spiritual discipline" to help them become givers more like God.*

Tithing is never mentioned so as not to scare members.

27. *All members are expected to participate in one ministry of the church each year based on their spiritual gifts and may continue working in that ministry as long as they have the gifts and passion for it.*

A few are nominated and elected each year to staff the church's committees for two- or three-year terms, after which they must leave that committee and be elected to another (for which they may or may not be gifted).

28. *A continuing ministry gifts program (church endowment fund) enables the congregation to be faithful stewards of their accumulated assets.*

The church does not have or want a church endowment fund so as not to hurt annual giving.

Christian Education

29. *The primary mission of Christian education is to disciple* all *members—adults, youth, children—in the way of Jesus.*

The primary mission of Christian education is to teach children the basic tenants of the faith.

30. *Every member is expected and encouraged to participate in at least one discipling opportunity each year, with a large percentage of them doing so.*

Most adults do not attend any form of adult education. Most youth disappear following their confirmation.

31. *A youth* ministry *is developed in which youth (ages twelve to eighteen) come to know Jesus and learn to follow in his footsteps. Social, "fun" events are part of this process.*

A youth *fellowship* schedules a series of social, "fun" events because that is all youth will attend.

32. *Ongoing, "hands-on" educational experiences for children ages two to eleven are developed (Sunday school, Wednesday family night, vacation Bible school, etc.), while using the eight methods of learning that pertains to meaningful, Christian life.*

A Sunday school for children uses a curriculum that is easy for the teachers, does not take too much time to prepare, and has the children listening to the teacher talk and participating in crafts not necessarily related to meaningful Christian life.

PASTORAL (CONGREGATIONAL) CARE

33. *Pastors train spiritually gifted laity to care for the members of the congregation.*

It is the pastor's job to do pastoral care!

WIDER MISSION

34. *The congregation is significantly monetarily invested and personally involved in being God's servants of God's children who are suffering throughout the world.*

The congregation has a low monetary investment and personal involvement beyond their own church.

35. *The congregation has a passion for enabling all of God's children to experience God's plan for this world of "shalom" (justice, peace, unity, prosperity).*

The congregation believes that Christians and churches should stay out of politics and social justice issues since they are divisive.

BUILDINGS AND PROPERTY

36. *The church buildings and property are seen as tools and servants of all the other ministries of the church.*

The church buildings and property are seen as ends in themselves, often becoming "sacred cows."

chapter two

The Basic Authority in the Church

LIVING CHURCHES	DYING CHURCHES
Jesus is the basic authority as	The congregation, council,
"the sole head of the church."	trustees, pastor, or a layperson
	is the basic authority.

IN THE THEOLOGICAL PREAMBLE OF MOST CHURCH constitutions, it states clearly, "Jesus is the sole head of the church!" After all, that is basic biblical theology! "He (Jesus) is the head of the body, the church; he is the beginning, the firstborn from the dead, so that he might come to have first place in everything" (Col. 1:18). Likewise, in 1 Corinthians 12:12–27, Paul also speaks of the church as the body of Christ in which all parts of the body must fulfill their unique tasks to enable the mission of the whole church to be accomplished. But that will happen only if all parts of the body are governed by Jesus, who is the "head" of the body. Moreover, in the first century of the church's existence, the only affirmation of faith a new believer needed to make to be baptized was, "Jesus is Lord!" And to affirm that Jesus was "Lord" meant that Jesus would be the ruler, the basic authority in that person's life.

However, following the theological preamble of United Church of Christ constitutions, usually in the very next section, it reads, "The congregation has the right of control in all its affairs." Is that contradictory? Can we have two basic authorities at the same time—Jesus and the congregation? Do you suppose our congregations ever out-vote Jesus—who is "the *sole head* of the church," the ruler of our lives?

What actually happens in most congregations is that we quickly ignore that first assertion that "Jesus is the sole head of the church" and operate solely from the perspective that "the congregation has the right of control in all its affairs." In some churches, it is not the congregation, but the church council/consistory, or the trustees, or the pastor, or the president/moderator, or one or more individuals within the congregation who have taken it upon themselves to "run things," whether or not they hold an elective position.

As Gamaliel cautioned his fellow Jewish high priests when they were about to kill Peter and some of the other apostles, "If this plan or this undertaking is of human origin, it will fail; but if it is of God, you will not be able to overthrow them—in that case you may even be found fighting against God!" (Acts 5:38–39). I suggest that one of the basic reasons most of our mainline churches are dying is that they have become "human constructs" in which church decisions are made out of human preferences, ideas, and understandings (via the congregation, church councils/consistories, committees, boards, and individuals), rather than "God constructs," that seek the will and the way of Jesus as decisions are made regarding the nature and mission of the church. In many ways our churches have been "fighting against God!"

The mainline churches that I see "making it" today are those that affirm Jesus as the basic authority, the sole head of the church. I know of one church, Ginghamsburg United Methodist Church in Ginghamsburg, Ohio, which has actually written into its church constitution that "no one may vote 'no' regarding something Jesus would want or do!" I am convinced that if all churches would do likewise, they would thrive today because nothing could defeat them!

But many within the church ask, "How do we know what Jesus wants us to do?" My answer is, "We would be forced to study the Bible when we are in the process of formulating and setting church policy. We would have to discover together what Jesus would want regarding the particular decisions with which we were faced. Imagine us doing Bible study in our congregational meetings and at gatherings of our church councils, consistories, committees, and boards! Would it make a major difference in what we decide to do or not do?

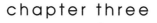

chapter three

Vision

LIVING CHURCHES

*There is a God-given vision
of the church's future.*

DYING CHURCHES

There is no vision of where
the church is going.

THE BIBLE SAYS, "Where there is no vision, the people perish!" (Prov. 29:18 KJV). Similarly, where there is no vision, churches perish! Often when I ask church members today, "What is going to happen in your church ten years from now?" The answer is, "Ten years from now this church will be gone!" I tell them, "If that is your vision, then you will consciously and subconsciously work toward that vision, and you will achieve it! However, if you obtain a new vision, one that God wants for your church, and open yourselves to the living Spirit of God/Jesus in the world, then God will energize you and help you fulfill your new vision!"

What is a vision for a church? A vision is a mental picture, an image, a concept, a new idea of what God/Jesus wants a particular church to be within its own unique setting. What will it look like? What will it be doing five to ten years into the future in the context of the new and rapidly changing world in which a church is now situated? Moreover, when God/Jesus provides a vision, it is BIG enough for God to fit into it, BIG enough that God/Jesus will have to help achieve it. We will constantly need God/Jesus revealing to us what the vision is and then guiding us toward it step by step, encouraging us, pushing us, pulling us, lifting us into the new vision. Thus, our new vision cannot and will not be "doing tomorrow what we are doing today." It will be a vision in which the church will be seeking to transform the present and the future according to God's ways as revealed in Jesus, rather than seeking to perpetuate a past which is gone and will never return.

When I help churches obtain a new God/Jesus–driven vision for their church, I lead them through a "Pentecost experience." When the disciples crept back into Jerusalem fifty days after the resurrection, their vision of the future of their movement had been shattered. Jesus—their leader, their visionary, their power and strength—had been arrested, tortured, and killed. He was gone! His vision of the realm of God being here on earth in which people could live today if they just obeyed God, their ruler, seemed to have disappeared. The realm must not have come in Jesus' lifetime and undoubtedly would not come in the future. Jesus' vision must have been a delusion!

Moreover, the disciples were terrified that his fate would be theirs if they did not stay hidden from view. So they entered Jerusalem incognito, hiding in a house with all of the windows shuttered and the doors locked. But then something like wind came into the room. Something was there that no one could see, but they could feel it; they were aware of its presence. In addition, the disciples experienced another sensation. Something like fire seemed to have come into the room, setting each one of them on "fire," a fire of excitement and enthusiasm! What was it? Peter proclaimed it to be what the prophet Joel had spoken of five hundred years earlier: "God declares, that I will pour out my Spirit upon all flesh, and your sons and your daughters shall prophesy, and your young men shall see visions, and your old men shall dream dreams" (Acts 2:17).

That's what happened on the first Pentecost! The Holy Spirit, the Spirit of the Living God/Jesus, came into that room of frightened, depressed, hopeless disciples who had given up on the vision that Jesus had given them. It was the Holy Spirit in the room that they could sense but could not see and it was the Holy Spirit who lit each of them on fire by giving them a renewed vision of the future of their movement!

What was that new vision? They were going to stop being afraid and hiding from the world!

Instead they were going to go out into the world, to every nation under heaven, and proclaim boldly that Jesus was alive, that he was the Christ (Messiah—the anointed one of God to rule and lead God's people), and therefore he was Lord, the one who needed to be obeyed in order to live in God's realm here on earth. Moreover, they were going to begin communities of Jesus' followers that would function as Jesus' body, his physical presence, doing Jesus' ministries here on earth. And with the powerful help of God/Jesus, they were going to do all this in their lifetimes. And it was accomplished!

People in small or even medium-sized churches often tell me, "But, there are too few of us in this congregation to have a big vision; too few of us to do something really significant." My response is, "There were only eleven disciples, but with the help of the Holy Spirit they achieved their seemingly impossible vision within their lifetimes (even though it cost each one his life). And so can you! After all, "for God all things are possible" (Matt. 19:26).

Thus, when I lead "visioning sessions" with churches, we invite God, the Holy Spirit, to come into the room as on Pentecost and give those assembled God's vision for their church ten years from now. We are not interested in their personal preferences, nor their particular desires or wants, but we want them to listen for the Holy Spirit's whisperings/shoutings in their ears and minds and, when they hear them, to holler them out so that I can record them on newsprint. We must remember that this church is *not our church* to do with as we please, but this is *Jesus' church* and we must seek Jesus' will, that of the Holy Spirit, rather than our own human constructs (preferences, wants, ideas, etc.).

I also remind those in visioning sessions, "Do not quench the Spirit" (1 Thess. 5:19). When a great vision for your church comes to you from the Holy Spirit, don't say to yourself, "I'd better not propose this because I know some in the congregation may not like it." That is to quench the Spirit! When the Spirit gives you a wonderfully creative new idea, don't say to yourself, "Oh, we couldn't afford that!" That is to quench the Spirit. Instead, when the Spirit of the Living Jesus gives you a vision, shout it out loudly and boldly as those first disciples did so long ago on Pentecost!

We usually fill up four to five pages of large-sized newsprint with what we hear from the Holy Spirit—and it's exciting, filling those in attendance with great enthusiasm for their new future. After all, the word "enthusiasm" comes from the Greek words, *"en theos,"* which means "in God." Yes, when we are filled with enthusiasm, we are "in God," and likewise, when we have no enthusiasm, we probably are not "in God." I know of nothing that fills people in churches with more excitement and enthusiasm than when they discern God's vision for their church in the future!

chapter four

Mission Statement and Strategies

LIVING CHURCHES	DYING CHURCHES
A clear, concise mission statement exists, with specific, concrete strategies to achieve that mission and vision.	No clear, concise mission statement exists, nor any specific, concrete strategies to achieve a mission and vision.

D ECLINING/DYING CHURCHES EITHER do not have a mission statement, or they have one that has been created by a large committee, resulting in a mission statement that is filled with generalized statements one or more long paragraphs in length, sometimes even a full page (in order to include something everyone on the committee wanted in some form or fashion). When I ask a group of leaders, including the pastor, from a church with this type of long committee-produced mission statement, "What is your mission statement?" usually not one person—not even the pastor—can tell me what it is. This happens even in those churches that have printed copies of their mission statement hanging on the walls of their church.

But most mainline Protestant churches have no mission statement whatsoever, even though almost every business or corporation today has a mission statement and reviews it every few years to see if it is still adequate for their rapidly changing environment. Many church people say, "Isn't the mission of the church always the same—yesterday, today, and tomorrow?" "Isn't it already included in our church's constitution?" (Although no one can tell you what their constitution says about it either!) I think it is fair to say that most mainline church members have no idea what the basic mission, task, or purpose of the church is other than knowing what they have been doing in the past. Thus, the mission of the church is to "Keep doing what we have been doing," even though that is causing the drastic decline in our churches since 1965 and is the primary cause of the impending death of our churches in the coming thirty years.

The best, most effective church mission statements I have seen or heard are clear, concise statements usually in three words or one phrase or one sentence. Frazier United Methodist Church in Montgomery, Alabama, has a three-word mission statement that I believe powerfully sums up the mission of the church and is easy to remember: "Win! Disciple! Serve!" meaning "Win people to Christ!" "Disciple them in the way of Christ!" "Serve the world in the name and Spirit of Christ!"

Another clear, concise, effective mission statement that sums up the mission of the body of Christ comes from the United Methodist Church of Ginghamsburg, Ohio. It is, "To know Jesus, and to make him known!" Messiah Lutheran Church of Yorba Linda, California, has adopted that same mission statement. A third effective mission statement is that of the First Congregational United Church of Christ in Longmont, Colorado, "Extending the Reach of Christ!" Each of these mission statements is easy to remember so that everyone in the church is able to know it, repeat it, and attempt to live up to it. Moreover, each of these mission statements is couched in simple, clear, concise language.

What is the purpose of an effective mission statement? A mission statement is the basic, most essential, task, purpose, and "business" of a particular church. It does not seek to describe everything that the church does, nor is it a compilation of the personal preferences, desires, wishes, or whims of all the members of the congregation. It is the *orders* that God/Jesus is giving to that church at this time in history in the context of its new and rapidly changing environment.

A procedure that I have found helpful for creating and drafting a mission statement with a group of church members is to begin with Bible study on the nature and mission of the church. (This might take several sessions.) Then following a prayer time when the Holy Spirit is asked to reveal to each of us the mission that God has for our church, ask each person to write down three words or one phrase or one sentence that each thinks best describes the basic mission, task, and purpose of this church as the body of Christ in the world today. The facilitator writes these down on newsprint, after which the group collates similar words/phrases/sentences into categories. The next step is to have each person write down three more words or one phrase/sentence from the categories that are left, and keep following this procedure until a mission statement is attained that has but three to five words, one phrase, or one sentence. Celebrate that achievement with songs of praise and thanksgiving, have it approved by the entire congregation, hang framed copies of it in bold print in every room in the church, print it weekly in Sunday bulletins and regularly in the church newsletter, and add it to your church's letterhead.

Such efforts enable the mission statement to be created and publicized, but thereafter, the primary function of the mission statement is that it needs to become the internal guidance system regarding what the church may and must do, as well as what the church may and must not do in its everyday life! How should the church be organized, what kind of structures are needed, what staff positions are necessary, what is being done now that needs to be retained, what needs to be changed, what needs to be dropped, what kind of space and facilities are required? The answers to these questions come from what the mission statement allows/requires the church to do in order to accomplish its mission and achieve its vision. If someone, some group, or some committee/ministry of the church recommends that the church begin a new program, the criterion for either doing it or not is "Does it fit the mission statement; does it help the church accomplish its basic task?" If so, and if the necessary financial resources are there or can be obtained, the answer is, "Bless you! Move ahead!" If a particular request does not aid the mission of the church as stated in the mission statement, the answer is, "We are sorry, but our mission statement doesn't allow us to do that!"

Some believe that a church's mission statement ought to be written in such a way as to be an advertising tool to be used outside the church. Although it is possible for a mission statement to be an effective evangelistic tool (and some are), that should *not* be the primary purpose of a mission statement, since we have seen that it is essentially an internal guidance system. If your mission statement will not work for effective evangelism, you might want to derive a motto from the mission statement that is more appropriate for external use.

After a church has asked for, received, and developed Jesus' vision for their church in the near future (which is the final result, the end product of accomplishing its mission), and after it has developed a clear, concise, effective mission statement (the basic purpose, task, and business the church will be about to reach the end result: its vision), then specific, concrete strategies need to be developed in each ministry of the church to accomplish its mission and move toward its vision. Strategies are specifically how and what we will do to accomplish our mission and achieve our vision.

The following are examples of vision and mission statements and strategies for ministries.

Vision: St. Paul's Church will be a growing, thriving, effective outpost of Jesus' ministries in its service region (a twenty minute drive by car in all directions) and beyond.

Mission Statement: (the basic way we will achieve our vision): "Win! Disciple! Serve!" "Win people for Christ! "Disciple Them in the Way of Christ!" "Serve the World in the Name and Spirit of Christ!"

Strategies

Worship Ministry: Add a contemporary service in addition to keeping our traditional service in order to attract the younger generations and the unchurched and dechurched in our service area.

Evangelism Ministry: Train all of our members to "bubble enthusiastically" about the joy and meaning they are finding in their lives in Christ Jesus and within our church to their individual networks of two hundred-plus people they already know, 50 to 60 percent of whom are unchurched or dechurched.

Congregational Care Ministry: Train ten "care callers" in ministering with the hospitalized and homebound, and begin a Stephen's Ministry in our church for one-on-one ministry with the hurting.

Christian Education Ministry: Begin a "Saturday school" in conjunction with the new contemporary service on Saturdays.

Youth Ministry: Begin two weekly Bible studies for both the younger and older youth; add a Christian rock band to the youth concerts currently being held monthly in our church's fellowship hall.

Adult Christian Education Ministry: Design and execute a comprehensive program on weekends/weeknights to help disciple all of our adults in the Spirit and way of Jesus utilizing Bible studies, classes, retreats, speakers, and audiovisuals.

Wider Mission Ministry:

Begin a shelter for the homeless once a week in our church and raise money to add a shower and washer/dryer so our guests can take showers and wash their clothes.

Stewardship Ministry:

1. Develop a comprehensive year-round biblical stewardship education program for all members via sermons, newsletter articles, adult discipling classes, Bible studies, etc.

2. Call ourselves "a tithing church" and encourage all of our members to be tithers or tithers-in-process.

3. Set our giving goals as follows:

    immediate goal—3 percent of household income,

    growth goal—5 percent of household income,

    ultimate goal—10 percent of household income.

Buildings and Grounds Ministry:

1. Renovate the fellowship hall for the new contemporary worship service, including the necessary audiovisual and sound equipment.

2. Add a shower and washer/dryer to fellowship hall for the homeless.

Staff:

Add the necessary part-time staff for the contemporary worship service: ministerial, music, drama, visuals/sound.

The preceding list describes concrete, specific strategies for St. Paul's Church to begin implementing its mission "Win! Disciple! Serve!" and to start moving toward achieving its vision for the future of becoming a "growing, thriving, effective outpost of Jesus' ministries within its service region and beyond."

It is recommended that every church hold a long-range planning retreat every other year to review its vision and mission statement and to determine if they are still relevant to what is happening in the service region. Every church should also set strategies for the next two years that are in accord with their mission statement and vision to give them the concrete, specific marching orders for their ministries until they regroup two years hence.

chapter five

Church Organization

LIVING CHURCHES

Church organization is based on a biblical model.

The church is organized according to ministries (worship/spiritual growth, evangelism, congregational care, Christian education, youth, wider mission, buildings and grounds, stewardship, and Christian witness in society.

All members are expected and encouraged to participate in one ministry of the church every year.

All members are led through a spiritual gifts inventory by a spiritual gifts ministry team to help all discern their God-given spiritual gifts, and members are "commanded" by God to use them in a related ministry.

Persons with spiritual gifts for certain ministries may continue to work in those ministries for as long as they have the gifts, sense a "calling" from God, and have passion for them.

DYING CHURCHES

Church organization is based on a human/democratic model.

The church is organized according to committees/boards (deacons, elders, trustees, worship, music, ushers, greeters, finance, fellowship, Christian education, memorial, etc.).

A few members are elected to committees/boards with two- to three-year terms. Thus, a small group provides leadership for the church.

Selected persons are recruited by a nominating committee, who too often seek people "who are breathing and who will say yes."

Members of committees are elected for a prescribed time (usually two to three years) after which they must stop and be elected to another committee for which they may or may not be gifted; or if they are not elected again, they may have to stop serving altogether.

Ministry teams gather to "do ministry" (plan/rehearse for worship; lead Bible studies; train people to evangelize; visit the unchurched, sick and homebound; teach children, youth, and adults; aid the homeless, build homes, feed the hungry, etc.).

Committee/board members meet primarily to "set policy," then go home and forget about it until next month when they gather to approve minutes, hear reports, and set more policy.

People who "do ministry" for which they are "gifted" tend to find satisfaction, excitement, genuine involvement, and fulfillment.

Committee/board members tend to "burn out," become bored, feel they are "going through the motions," and "wasting their valuable time"— and attendance lags.

Persons engaged in "ministry" are participating as "servants," obeying the call of God, who commands them to use their spiritual gifts in correlating ministries.

Committee/board members see themselves as "volunteers" (they choose to do this, or at *least allow themselves to be elected*).

IT IS READILY APPARENT that the two forms of church organization compared in the preceding list (ministries versus committees) have different beginning points (a biblical model versus a human model of nominations and elections), a completely different way of operating a church, a different level of involvement of parishioners (all members expected to be involved versus a few), a different level of trust in God and people (trusting all members as capable of leadership and sharing responsibility with all versus keeping control of the church in the hands of a few and not allowing anyone to solidify power and control by limiting the service of members in any one area to two to three years), and different results (growing/living churches versus declining/dying churches).

Following is a form of organization that is working today in mainline Protestant churches utilizing ministries rather than committees/boards. This type of organization is enabling mainline churches to become revitalized and grow again by aiding ministry rather than hindering it.

JESUS CHRIST
(The sole head of the Church)

CONGREGATION
(The right of control under the authority of Jesus)

pastor
church officers

one rep. from
each ministry

CHURCH COUNCIL/CABINET/CONSISTORY
(Coordinates, communicates between ministries; evaluates and provides for long-range planning; sets major policies between congregational meetings; monitors the budget)

Ministries

WORSHIP/SPIRITUAL GROWTH
(IN TEAMS)

1. worship services
   • service planning, scheduling
   • sacraments
   • flowers, banners, symbols
   • music, choirs, praise teams, bands, drama, dance, visuals, sound, lighting
2. spiritual growth groups
   • Bible studies, prayer groups
   • study/caring/sharing groups

Committees

Pastor-Parish Relations

Finance

Nominating (ad hoc)
   • For church officers and committees only

Budget (ad hoc) one rep. from each ministry, pastor, moderator, one rep. from finance committee

Audit (ad hoc)

Groups

Women's Organization

Men's Organization

Singles

Couples

(Other Groups)

Evangelism (in teams)

- evangelism education/training of congregation.
- publicity
- hospitality
- recruitment/visitor follow-up
- orientation of new members
- assimilation of new members
- inactive member follow-up

Congregational Care (in teams)

- calling on hospitalized/homebound
- transportation corps
- flowers, meals, cards
- support groups
- Stephen's Ministry
- Christian fellowship events (could be separate ministry)

Christian Education (in teams)

- selection/evaluation of Christian education staff
- Sunday/Saturday church school
- Vacation church school
- youth ministries (can be a separate ministry)
- adult discipling education
- teacher recruitment/training
- curriculum/supplies/etc.
- church educational resource center (library)

WIDER MISSION (IN TEAMS)

- community/area mission (homeless, food pantries, Habitat for Humanity, etc.)
- state, national, worldwide missions via denomination and/or on own
- support for missionaries, individuals, families
- Christian witness in society (education/action on systemic social change; this can a be a separate ministry)

BUILDINGS AND GROUNDS (IN TEAMS)

- maintenance (preventive, immediate, long-range)
- remodeling projects
- major capital needs
- maintenance staff

STEWARDSHIP (IN TEAMS)

- stewardship education of the congregation
- spiritual gifts (aids all members in discerning their spiritual gifts and participation in ministry)
- annual spiritual/stewardship growth events (pledge campaigns)
- Continuing Ministry Gifts (endowment fund)
- memorials

Among the distinguishing characteristics of this model of church organization are the following:

Jesus Christ is the "sole head of the Church!" He is the basic authority of the church rather than human beings in the form of the congregation, the church council/cabinet/consistory/elders/ trustees/finance committee or some self-selected individuals who have seized the power to "call the shots" from behind the scenes. When decisions must be made by the congregation or the Church Council, ministries, and remaining committees, they should undertake Bible study to determine what Jesus would want or do in a given situation, rather than making decisions on the basis of human personal preferences, ideas, conveniences, desires, wants, or whims.

The primary purpose of this biblically oriented model of governance is for the church to be the body of Christ in the world today by doing the ministry of Jesus rather than developing and maintaining structures primarily to guard against the sinfulness of humankind by allowing too much power to be placed in some hands for too long a time. Therefore, in our current forms of church governance, terms are limited and people are kept moving from one committee to another to avoid concentrations of power. Yet, most of us are aware that in spite of all of our attempts to avoid concentrations of power, it still happens frequently within our current organizations. Some maintain that the real reason for limiting terms of service on committees is to allow other church members to become involved in the leadership of the church. However, we all know that in most churches it is most often the same people who keep circulating from one committee to the next. Moreover, in the biblical model in which every member is expected to participate in ministry every year, there is no need to get other people involved. Most everyone already is!

The role of the church council/cabinet/consistory is *not* to be the controlling/power group in the church, but to promote and aid the coordination of the ministries and communication between them. It develops evaluation procedures and arranges annual and long-range planning for what is in the best interests of this entire body of Christ. It does not see, approve, or pay all the bills, although it does monitor the total budget on a monthly basis. It does not make decisions for the ministries, although it does participate in making decisions involving several of the ministries and approves new ministry initiatives that involve one or more ministries upon their recommendations. Moreover, the church council/cabinet/consistory is the steward of the mission statement that is the internal guidance system and authority for what the church may or may not do. Thus, the basic criterion for deciding what new or different initiatives may be undertaken is, "Is it in accord with our church's mission statement?" If it is, "Go to it!" If it is not, then "Sorry, it doesn't fit the mission statement!"

All members are expected and encouraged to participate in one ministry of the church for which they have the God-given spiritual gifts. It is the responsibility of the spiritual gifts team of the stewardship ministry to aid all current and new members in discerning their spiritual gifts aided by a spiritual gifts inventory and a chart revealing the church's ministries that correlate to the particular biblical spiritual gifts. The spiritual gifts team encourages the participation of every member in ministry as a matter of the stewardship of his or her God-given gifts.

Each of the ministry teams has its own budget (its portion of the entire church budget) and authorizes expenditures from it as long as they stay within the church budget. If they wish to overspend their budget, they must receive the church council's approval to do so. If in monitoring the church budget, the church council sees a need to cut spending by a certain percentage during a given year, the ministries decide where and how their budgets will be cut.

The church budget is not prepared by the trustees, buildings and grounds committee, finance committee, or the church council. The budget committee is chaired by the church moderator/president and made up of one representative from each of the ministries, one representative from the finance committee, and the pastor. Each of the ministry representatives brings its ministry's budget requests to the committee emanating from their mission and strategies for the next year. The stewardship ministry representative brings that ministry's best estimate of the anticipated income for the next year. If it appears that the budget requests will need to be cut, then the ministries make the cuts to bring back to the budget bommittee. Thus, together, the ministries that plan the work of the church, and ask for, receive, and use the monies are also involved in preparing and recommending the church budget to the church council and congregation for approval.

There are only two standing committees that meet throughout the year and report to the church council—pastor-parish relations and finance. There are three ad hoc committees that meet only as the need arises (budget, audit, and nominating). The nominating committee nominates only the church officers and the members of the standing and ad hoc committees to the congregation. Ministry participants are recruited from the work of the spiritual gifts team, which seeks to encourage all members of the church to participate in one ministry for which they have the necessary spiritual gifts.

The role of the pastor is not the old model of the pastor doing all the ministries of the church (worship, evangelism, pastoral/congregational care, all Bible studies, youth ministry) while the laity help the pastor (preparing, serving, and washing dishes for communion; supplying flowers for the altar; handling finances; maintaining buildings and grounds; and setting policies of the church, including setting policies for the pastor). Instead, the role of the pastor is to help the congregation to know Jesus, disciple them in Jesus' way, and equip the saints for ministry, which means to equip the laity of the church to do the ministries of the church. Again, it is a biblical model rather than a human-created model.

The purpose of the pastor-parish relations committee is not primarily that of trying to "shape up" the pastor according to anonymous grievances of some parishioners. The role of this committee is to act as a support group for the pastor, discussing with the pastor his/her mission of equipping the saints for ministry, hearing him/her out on his/her dreams, evaluations, concerns, problems, and possibilities; sharing the names and concerns that certain members have about the pastor and his/her ministry, as well as helping to develop communication and reconciliation between the pastor and these persons.

chapter six

Roles of Pastor(s) and Staff

LIVING CHURCHES	DYING CHURCHES
The role of pastor(s) is to "equip the saints" for ministry to enable all members to do ministry.	The pastor(s)/staff are paid to do the ministries of the church, while the laity "set policy" and perform the more "secular" tasks.
The church seeks to build the staff as quickly as possible to keep providing more ministries for more people.	The church seek to keep the staff at a bare minimum to keep costs down.

A TYPICAL MAINLINE PROTESTANT CHURCH constitution reads as follows: "It shall be the duty of the pastor(s) to conduct worship services, direct the work of religious education, administer the Holy Sacraments, visit the sick, comfort the distressed, seek new members, and perform all such duties as belong to the pastor's office." In other words, a pastor has the responsibility to perform the basic ministries of the church, namely, planning and leading worship (with the help of one or two other staff, the organist and choir director), visiting the hospitalized and homebound, directing the Christian education ministry (usually including working with the youth and leading all or most adult Bible studies and classes), counseling with those in need, and calling upon potential new members.

The laity see their role as primarily that of "setting policy" for the church, the pastor(s), other staff, and the ministries through the various committees and boards on which they serve, as well as helping the pastor(s) by performing the more "secular" tasks with which they feel most comfortable, such as administration; maintaining the buildings and grounds; preparing/serving the sacraments and washing the dishes thereafter; providing flowers for the altar; creating and monitoring the budgets and handling the finances; and planning and executing church fellowship events, church dinners, potluck suppers, and rummage sales. The church described above is a declining/dying church!

Moreover, this same church seeks to keep the staff to the barest minimum in order to keep costs down. If the church is having financial problems (which almost all churches encounter on a regular basis), the first quick response is to cut staff rather than to seek to have their people become better stewards and give more of their abundance to strengthen the ministries of their church. When a church cuts staff, it cuts Jesus' ministries and cuts the possibilities of reaching more people to bring them to Christ and his way. It is on a rapid downward cycle! It is a declining/dying church!

On the other hand, in a growing/living church the primary role of a pastor is to turn church members into disciples of Jesus and followers of his way, and then to equip the saints (all the members of the church) for doing ministry, rather than the pastor(s) doing the ministries while the laity set policy and handle the more "secular" activities of the church (see Eph. 4:11–13).

That is what Paul did when he started churches throughout present-day Turkey and Greece. He helped people come to know Jesus, to follow his way, and trained them to continue the ministries he performed with the people of their region. This means that pastors are to teach and train the laity about *what* the ministries of the church are, *why* they need to be done, and *how* to do them rather than to spend most of their time doing the ministries themselves and keeping the laity from doing ministry, thereby denying them the opportunity of fulfilling their biblical roles of being priests (1 Pet. 2:9).

Thus, in the growing/living church the laity are taught and trained in the ministry of *worship* by:

1. Being on various worship teams (planning, praise, band, choirs, drama, visuals, sound/lighting);

2. Participating in the *ministry of evangelism* on various teams (evangelism education/training, publicity, hospitality, recruitment, orientation, assimilation, and inactive member follow-up);

3. Doing the *ministry of congregational care* on teams—such as hospital/homebound calling, transportation corps, Stephen's Ministry, support groups, providing meals/cards/flowers, fellowship opportunities;

4. Participating in the *ministry of Christian education* on teams—such as teaching children, working with youth, vacation church school, leading Bible studies and other adult classes, church resource center, audiovisuals;

5. Getting involved in the *ministry of wider mission* via teams—such as working with food pantries, shelters for the homeless, Habitat for Humanity; mentoring persons moving from homelessness into independent living; tutoring; overseas missions;

6. Engaging in the *ministry of stewardship* on the teams of stewardship education, spiritual gifts, annual stewardship/ spiritual growth events (campaigns), continuing ministry gifts (endowment fund); memorial gifts;

7. Participating in the *ministry of buildings and grounds* on the teams of preventive, immediate, and long-term maintenance (grounds beautification, remodeling, planning additions or a relocation).

Moreover, a growing/living church is always planning ahead regarding the addition of more staff so that more ministry education and training of more laity can take place through their church to enable more people outside the church to know Jesus and his way, become discipled, and become servants of others. They realize that it is difficult for a church to add a full-time staff person in any given year, so they perhaps start by offering an honorarium to a person with the necessary spiritual gifts, then moving that person to quarter-time, then to half-time, and so on. Moreover, that new staff person in many instances need not be an ordained person (depending on whether or not seminary training is required). Today in fact, most seminary students are trained as generalists rather than specialists.

chapter seven

Expectations of Church Membership

LIVING CHURCHES	DYING CHURCHES
High expectations lead to	Low expectations lead to
high results!	low results!

MOST MAINLINE PROTESTANT CHURCHES have low expectations of their members' involvement. I have seen many church constitutions that read as follows: "A member who for a period of two years or more has not attended the church's worship, or contributed to its support, or partaken of communion shall have that person's membership status reviewed by the membership committee."

In other words, as long as a church member attends at least one service every two years, makes any kind of a financial offering over a two- year period, and participates in communion at least once every two years, that person is considered a member in good standing. That is all that is expected of members in these churches. And, too often, that is what they get!

One church constitution I came across recently even read as follows:

"Each member shall be responsible for the following:

1. Attend worship services if physically able.

2. Provide a minimum of financial support each calendar year. This is not required if this proves to present a financial hardship.

3. Provide the church office with any change of address."

This church is even recommending that its members make a "minimum" financial contribution, and one of three membership requirements is simply "let us know if you move!" These churches are declining/dying churches!

On the other hand, growing/living churches have high expectations of their memberships, such as "We expect our members to attend worship regularly; participate in a spiritual growth group/discipling class/Bible study, etc; serve in a ministry of the church for which they have the spiritual gifts; be a tither or tither-in-process." And these high expectations are not just for one year, but for every year they are members of the church.

Immediately, mainline Protestants declare that these types of high expectations would be impossible for their churches, because they are having difficulty in getting their members to fulfill the low expectations they have for their members now. They wouldn't have any members at all if they asked for anything more from their people.

But, that is just the point! High expectations of church members lead to high results, whereas low expectations lead to low results! The churches today that have low expectations are declining/dying churches. On the other hand, those mainline churches with high expectations of their membership are growing in membership and worship attendance, in the multiplication of their ministries and participation in them, in financial stability, and, most importantly, they are achieving their mission and vision of extending the reach of Christ in our world today.

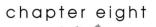

chapter eight

Evangelism

LIVING CHURCHES	DYING CHURCHES
Evangelism is considered the primary mission of the church.	Evangelism has not been engaged in the last fifty years, or at best is low on the priority scale.
Evangelism is engaged in to enable all to live under the reign of God on earth for their own well-being and that of the whole world.	New members are sought to help pay the bills and staff the church's committees.
All members of the church are expected to participate in the ministry of evangelism.	Evangelism is the work of the pastor and evangelism committee (if there is one).
Each ministry of the church needs to have an evangelistic thrust.	All committees of the church are separate and each does its own work.

E VANGELISM IS THE PRIMARY MISSION of the church. Our Bibles maintain clearly that evangelism (sharing the good news of life under the reign of God in the Spirit of Jesus within the community of God's people) is the *primary mission* of God's chosen people. This message is found throughout the entirety of our Bibles, from Genesis through the New Testament. Here it is in brief form:

When most all the people on earth had rebelled against God's authority, had taken control of their own lives and were doing as they pleased ("the wickedness of humanity was great in the earth, and . . . every inclination of the thoughts of their hearts was only evil," Gen. 6:5), God chose a people, not because they were more spiritual or more moral than others, but because God had a task, a mission for them to accomplish, to "be a blessing" to all people by bringing them back under God's authority for their own well-being and that of the whole world (salvation) (Gen. 12:1–2).

God's chosen people, however (for the most part), refused to perform that mission. An example is Jonah refusing to go to Nineveh to encourage its two hundred thousand inhabitants to obey God's ways, because he felt his mission was to improve the "quality" of the faith of the chosen people rather than be concerned with "quantity" elsewhere. So God punished Jonah until he did as God commanded, because God loved the people of Nineveh even as God loved the Hebrews.

Finally, God sent Jesus of Nazareth to proclaim the good news (evangel) of the current presence and future fulfillment of the reign of God on earth (Mark 1:15); to free people of their enslavements, which kept them from obeying God; to make them whole again by enabling them to live once again under God's authority. (Matt. 4:23).

However, since Jesus could not reach everyone on earth by himself, he first called twelve disciples to "fish for people," catching them by the "netful" for life under God's reign (Matt. 4:19). Then Jesus sent seventy others out to do the same (Luke 10:1–12). And finally, Jesus told all of his followers of his time and those in the future to "go therefore and make disciples of all nations" (Matt. 28:19).

In the first century of the Christian church's existence the primary mission and activity of its people was to "be my witnesses in Jerusalem, in all of Judea and Samaria, and to the ends of the earth" (Acts 1:8). To fulfill this task, they were empowered by the Holy Spirit (Acts 1:8); "spoke the word of God with boldness" (Acts 4:31); "[could not] stop speaking about what [they] have seen and heard"(Acts 4:20); even gladly went to prison and to their deaths in order to proclaim the Good News of life in Christ Jesus and in his church communities (Acts 7).

The result? The good news (evangel) of Jesus and life under the reign of God was spread and the church of Jesus Christ was begun throughout the entire known world with thousands coming back under God's authority within the lifetime of the first century evangelists!

Thus, it is clear that the primary task/mission of the chosen people throughout the entire Bible, from the time of Abraham to the followers of Jesus in the first century, was that of evangelism, reaching out to all of God's children everywhere in order to enable them to live under God's rule for their own well-being and that of the entire world (salvation) by sharing the good news (evangel) of life under God (which is heaven) as opposed to life ruled by any other person, philosophy, nation, ideology, or when individual humans deify themselves and do as they please (which is hell).

Yet in spite of this, most mainline Protestant churches have not engaged in the ministry of evangelism over the past fifty years, which is sheer rebellion, gross disobedience against God's will! Why not? Partly because fifty years ago mainline Protestant churches didn't need to evangelize. People just fell into their doors, and we thought this would go on forever!

Fifty years ago Christendom seemed to reign. The church was at the center of our society. It was the acceptable thing to do to go to church on Sunday mornings. If people didn't go to church back then, others thought there was something wrong with them. They were looked down upon. In fact, some went to church every Sunday, even though they fell asleep shortly after they arrived and stayed asleep until they went home, but they would be back the next week to sleep again—because they were fulfilling their God-given duty to go to church! Moreover, fifty years ago the church was at the center of our social life. That's where you met people, often your future spouse, and made many lifelong friends.

When most of the soldiers came home from World War II, were married, and had babies—lots of babies, eighty million of them over the next twenty years (the baby boomer generation)—most of them and their families were baptized and confirmed in the church, because it was the thing to do in our culture. That's why in the 1950s and early 1960s churches were enlarging their sanctuaries and building Christian education facilities. But since 1965 most of the baby boomers have left the churches, joining the rapidly growing ranks of the so-called dechurched (once active, but no longer). And most of their children, "generation X," haven't even been baptized; many have never stepped foot in a church except to attend a wedding or a funeral.

So churches didn't have to do evangelism fifty years ago. We thought we had better ideas than God or Jesus! But even as the mainline churches began declining in the mid-1960s (most are still declining), mainline church folk developed very sophisticated arguments why evangelism wasn't a good thing to do by the church. Following are some of those arguments against evangelism with biblical responses:

ARGUMENT NO. 1

We don't like the word "evangelism." It has connotations of manipulative television evangelists. We don't want to be like the fundamentalists who turn so many off by asking strangers if they have been saved and threatening eternal hell if they don't respond affirmatively.

BIBLICAL RESPONSES

Jesus said, "Do not judge, so that you may not be judged" (Matt. 7:1–5). Jesus said, "The harvest is plentiful, but the laborers are few" (Matt. 9:37).

We don't have to do evangelism like the fundamentalists, but are we so busy criticizing them that we do little or nothing at all? Actually, our stereotypes are badly outdated! The churches that are growing today (including the evangelical churches) no longer use those old methods, because they no longer work.

The word "evangelism" is the very basis of our Christian faith and mission. It means "gospel," "good news." Spreading the good news of life in the Spirit of Jesus and in his church was and is the primary message and mission of the church of Jesus Christ, except in those periods when the church was decaying and dying—such as now!

ARGUMENT NO. 2

"We don't have a right to "lay our trip" on someone else. We are tolerant people who leave everyone free to think and believe for themselves!

BIBLICAL RESPONSES

Jesus said, "Follow me, and I will make you fish for people" (Matt. 4:19)—and in those days they fished with nets, not single hooks! Jesus said, "Go, therefore, and make disciples of all nations" (Matt. 28:19).

We are to "lay our trip" on others, not by telling them what to believe or how to live, but we by sharing the good news (the joy, meaning, and fulfillment) that we have experienced in our lives in Christ Jesus with as many as possible when the situations present themselves.

ARGUMENT NO. 3

It is not good for churches to become too large. You will no longer know everyone. The warmth and friendliness will be exchanged for a cold impersonalism. Let's just get enough new members to replace the ones we lose to help us pay the bills.

BIBLICAL RESPONSES

On the day of Pentecost Peter said, "Repent, and be baptized every one of you in the name of Jesus Christ, so that your sins may be forgiven; and you will receive the gift of the Holy Spirit. . . . So those who welcomed his message were baptized, and that day about three thousand persons were added to their number" (Acts 2:38, 41).

Should Peter and the disciples have refused to baptize those three thousand folk who came to Christ so that they wouldn't lose their warmth and friendliness? Was it possible to have a close-knit fellowship with three thousand? Listen: "They spent their time in learning from the apostles, taking part in the fellowship, and sharing in the fellowship meals and prayers. All the believers continued together in close fellowship, even sharing their belongings with each other" (Acts 2:42, 44 GNB).

ARGUMENT NO. 4

We should strive for quality in our churches, rather than quantity, and the quality suffers as the quantity increases. We need to spend our efforts at improving the quality of the Christian faith and life of our members before we work at getting more members.

BIBLICAL RESPONSE

Read the story of Jonah. He used this same argument when God sent him to Nineveh (to strangers and enemies) to preach repentance and bring them back under God's authority for their own well-being and that of the whole world. Jonah argued that he felt his mission was to increase the quality of the faith of the chosen people in Judah rather than being concerned about the "quantity," the 200,000 people in Nineveh. Besides, they were such evil people, God should just let them reap the consequences of their evil deeds, and leave him free to develop the "quality" of the Judeans. But God had a whale swallow him until he was ready to do as God wanted and commanded!

Quality of faith and the quantity of persons brought into God's realm are not antithetical! They are both important and must be worked on simultaneously.

ARGUMENT NO. 5

Actions speak louder than words. We just need to have inspiring worship, a good Christian education program, youth ministries, and other interesting programs, and people will be attracted to us, visit us, be impressed, and join with us. We need not reach out to them with words! Evangelism by actions is sufficient!

Jesus sent out the twelve saying, "Go rather to the lost sheep of the house of Israel. As you go, proclaim the good news, 'The kingdom of heaven has come near.' Cure the sick, raise the dead, cleanse the lepers, cast out demons" (Matt. 10:6–8a).

"But you will receive power when the Holy Spirit has come upon you; and you will be my witnesses in Jerusalem, in all Judea and Samaria, and to the ends of the earth" (Acts 1:8).

We need to engage in Acts evangelism and Word evangelism simultaneously. Of course, we must live our faith, or "walk the talk." But we must also talk! Should we engage in meeting human need without telling others why we do this or without inviting them to participate in our faith community so that they in turn can help others? When fishing for people on behalf of God's realm, it's not enough to put out the bait. We also need to set the hook!

The symbol of the Garden Grove Community Church (the Crystal Cathedral) in California is a shepherd's staff with a fishhook in it. A church needs to meet needs and heal hurts in the name and spirit of Jesus (the shepherd's staff), but also be willing to set the hook, namely, catch those who are helped for life in Christ's realm here on earth, so they, too, will learn to become servants of others in the name and Spirit of Jesus!

Thus, because mainline Protestant churches didn't need to do evangelism fifty years ago and have developed a number of sophisticated arguments against doing evangelism at all, we haven't been doing evangelism, we don't know how, and we really don't want to do it!

How Not to Do Evangelism

Yet, since most of our churches have been experiencing significant losses of membership and funding, as well as having great difficulty in obtaining enough people to serve on the churches' many committees, increasingly our church councils/consistories/cabinets have been hearing, "We need to get some new members to help us pay our bills and staff our committees. There aren't enough of us around anymore! We need a pastor who will get out and get us some new members. Maybe we can get a small membership committee together as well to give the pastor some help!"

There are several serious problems with that approach! First and foremost, the main purpose/mission of a ministry of evangelism is *not* to get new members to help us pay the bills and staff committees of our church. The mission of the church is not to add scalps to our belts! The mission/purpose of the church is to reach out to all people to enable them to experience the good news of life in Christ Jesus under the rule of God for their own well-being and that of the whole world. As Bill Easum says, "We are about Kingdom-work, not church-work!"[1]

Secondly, the ministry of evangelism is *not* the job of the pastor and a membership committee (if there is one), or solely the work of the pastor if there is not such a committee. Growing/living churches expect and train all members of the church to engage in the ministry of evangelism, since all are followers of Jesus who have been called by Jesus to "become fishers of people" and to catch people by the netful to live under the reign of God in the Spirit of Jesus within his communities of followers.

Thirdly, a membership committee or church growth committee is not an evangelism ministry! A membership or church growth committee is one that solely seeks to add members to the church. That is too narrow, too superficial, too small! An evangelism ministry is one that seeks to share the good news (evangel) of life in the Spirit of Jesus under God's rule, which will transform that person's life, not just add one more number to the church rolls.

Develop a "Ministry of Evangelism"

Give all your members a "spiritual gift inventory" to enable them to discern their biblical spiritual gifts and invite all who have the gift of evangelism (a passion to share the good news, joy, meaning, and significance they are experiencing in their life in Christ Jesus and in his church under the rule of God) to participate in the

---

ministry of evangelism in your church. Also, invite all who have the biblical spiritual gift of hospitality to join this ministry (these people are warm, friendly, outgoing, and not afraid or cautious of strangers).

Ask these folks to make this their primary ministry in the church over the next three years. Then, if they find this ministry meaningful and fulfilling, they may continue working in this ministry as long as they like. The pastor or other staff member works closely with this ministry as a resource person and coach.

Obviously, this is quite a different approach than our current modus operandi of electing people to an evangelism committee who are breathing and said "yes" to a friend on the nominating committee, and who, after a term of two to three years, must leave that committee and work in another whether or not they have the gifts for either one.

Basic Evangelism Strategies Working in Mainline Churches Today

EVERY MEMBER EVANGELISM

This is the most effective evangelism strategy that works today in all churches. Growing churches receive 70 to 90 percent of their new members this way. Each person in the church has a network of at least two hundred people with whom they are acquainted (family, friends, neighbors, working colleagues, those with whom they find recreation, etc), 50 to 60 percent of whom are unchurched (never connected) or dechurched (once active, but no longer).

All members are encouraged and trained to "bubble enthusiastically" about their life in Christ Jesus and in his church with these people they already know when the opportunities present themselves in their everyday lives.

We do this with our networks of acquaintances about all kinds of things. When we read a good book, we exclaim to our work colleague, "Did I read a good book!" That person may become interested because of our enthusiasm and ask to borrow our copy, which we are pleased to lend. That is sharing good news about a book. We "bubble enthusiastically" with others we know when we have seen a good movie or television show or traveled to some interesting place or had a fantastic meal at a restaurant. But, we "mainliners" do not do it regarding our faith or church!

Why not? Because our culture has instructed us that there are three things we may not talk about with those we know—religion, politics, and money! Therefore, we dutifully obey our culture and disobey our Lord Jesus by not talking about politics and money, much less "bubbling enthusiastically" about our faith and church. But, if we may not talk about money, we cannot engage in the ministry of stewardship! If we may not talk about politics, we cannot participate in the ministry of Christian social action, and if we may not talk about our religion, we cannot do the ministry of evangelism. I suggest that is why mainline churches do little, if anything, with these three crucial, but most neglected, ministries of the Christian church!

Churches that practice "every member evangelism" are known as "contagious churches"[2] because the enthusiasm and exuberance demonstrated by their members is quickly caught by those to whom they speak. Many of the listeners want what those people have.

SERVANT EVANGELISM

Servant evangelism was developed by a Baptist pastor and his people in Cincinnati, Ohio. Thinking that the former ways of doing evangelism in the Baptist tradition were outdated and no longer viable, he and some of the leaders of his congregation decided they would "do random acts of kindness with no strings attached" for the people of Cincinnati. Thus, they planned a series of "random acts of kindness" such as car washes, washing car windshields, and wrapping Christmas presents at shopping malls. Now, many churches do things like this—to make money for their church. But this church engaged in these activities for no charge.

I heard the pastor tell the story about their first car wash. Several weeks in advance, through the newspapers they announced a free car wash at their church on an upcoming Saturday morning. A cab driver stopped and asked, "What's the catch? There's no such thing as a free lunch!" They told him, "There is no catch! We'll wash your cab at no cost whatsoever!" He countered, "You'll probably ask for a donation afterwards, I imagine!" Their response was, "We don't accept donations!" So, he warily allowed them to wash his taxi. When they were through, they simply gave him a small card that said, "This is an example of God's love for you—with no strings attached!" On the other side of the card was the name of the church, address, phone number, and e-mail address. His response was "This is great! I'll hold the sign out by the road for you!" And as he did, he loudly proclaimed to cars going by, "This is for real! It's free, it's really free!" This church received ten thousand members over the next ten years and is known as the church that does all those wonderful, free things for the people of Cincinnati!

SMALL GROUP INVOLVEMENT

This is a method for reaching the unchurched of our time. It consists of developing a number of small groups, most of which are totally secular, with some based on sports activities, such as, jogging, volleyball, softball, bicycling, mountain climbing, and hiking. Then there are other groups based on service opportunities, such as car repair, working in soup kitchens, restoring old houses for poor people, and reading for the blind, as well as spiritual growth groups.

A trained church member or two or more in each group has the role of developing genuine, caring relationships with the unchurched in the group. After spending several months or a year in that group, they might invite their newfound friends to join them in a service group, or a Bible study group as well as inviting them to attend with them one of the church's contemporary worship services that would match their musical tastes. Thus, based on the development of genuine, caring relationships, the unchurched folk are gently and carefully led into the community of faith.

A fourth crucial and most effective strategy for evangelism in mainline Protestant churches today is, as Bill Easum has described so eloquently, "indigenous" worship3, namely, that which is couched in the language, music, and technology of the people we are trying to reach—the majority of the baby boomers who have left the church, and most of generation X who have never been connected to the church.

Missionaries in foreign lands find it necessary to communicate with the indigenous peoples in their own languages, with their own music, and in the context of their own technologies. Martin Luther insisted that for Christianity to be meaningful for the German people its worship had to be communicated in the German language rather than in Latin, in their music as opposed to Gregorian chants, and utilizing the contemporary technology of the printing press to enable the Bible to be read and the hymns to be sung by the German people themselves rather than just by the priests and choirs. So today we must reach and communicate with the younger generations in their language, with their music, and utilizing the technologies with which they have grown up, namely, television, the computer, video, electronic instruments, and multimedia.

I know there are some who oppose the use of worship for the purposes of evangelism, insisting that worship should have but one purpose, and one purpose alone, that of "glorifying God." But I maintain that one of the best ways we have of glorifying God is to obey the God who commanded the chosen people to "be a blessing" to the rest of the world by reaching out to all peoples and bringing them back under the reign of God. We should obey our Lord Jesus Christ, who called his followers to become "fishers of people" catching them by the netful for life under the rule of God here on this earth, as well as commanding all his followers at that time and for all time to "go to all people everywhere making them my disciples."

To attempt to reach out to all people by communicating with them in their own language, music, and technology is indeed to "glorify God." On the other hand, to insist that we must reach out to the younger generations and communicate with them only in the language, music, and technologies of our older generations (since these have been "baptized" by the older generations as "sacred") is to glorify ourselves and our traditions, rather than God.

Major Tasks of the Ministry of Evangelism

Create long-term goals, strategies, and budgets for the ministry of evangelism (initial budget goal: 5 percent of church budget) as well as conducting annual evaluations.

EVERY MEMBER EVANGELISM

Help identify and invite persons with the biblical, spiritual gifts of evangelism and hospitality to engage in the ministry of evangelism. Develop year-round evangelism education and training of the congregation regarding the biblical basis of evangelism and how to participate in every member evangelism.

PUBLICITY

Get the good news out to the public about life in the Spirit of Jesus and in this particular church of his followers. Blanket your church's service area—a twenty minute drive by car in all directions. Take out an ad in the telephone book yellow pages (in bold letters with a box around it). This is the first place people who are seeking a church look when moving into a new location.

Develop newspaper ads and stories about people and events (not just sermon titles and times of services), and "blow-ins" in local newspapers before Christmas and Easter.

Develop brochures about your church, including separate brochures regarding each ministry—Christian education of children, youth, and adults; wider mission; youth ministry; worship and music ministries, and other ministries your church may be doing.

Send letters to people moving into the area, letters to first- and second-time guests and "baby" letters written to parents of new babies in your service area.

Use door hangers, e-mail, radio spots, television, and radio or television coverage of worship services, if possible.

HOSPITALITY

Be a warm and welcoming community! Provide helpful signage to newcomers both outside and inside your building. Make an assessment of the hospitality of your buildings and grounds (are they inviting, warm, welcoming, functional, helpful?). Have reserved parking for guests only (closest to the church after the handicapped parking).

Have greeters and welcomers at the doors of the church. Greeters give a warm welcome to each person; welcomers look for every strange face and provide a warm welcome. If newcomers have children, welcomers show them where the church school rooms are, explain whether the children attend worship first, and so on. If newcomers are young couples with children, welcomers introduce them to other young couples; if single, introduce them to singles; if older, introduce them to the older members. Introduce all visitors and newcomers to the pastor and invite them to the social hour.

Set up an information booth or table with various brochures about your church and have someone there to answer questions, sign-up sheets for various events, and tapes of the services for sale with other materials. Provide guest name tags at the information table and in pews with information cards. Encourage all your church members to wear name tags so all can call each other by name.

Use "friendship folders" in worship, which all are asked to sign. Encourage guests to give addresses, phone numbers, and e-mail addresses. Pass them down the pews so that current members can see who the guests are in their pew and greet them warmly. The Sunday bulletin should have a whole page welcoming guests and providing helpful information for them. The pastor should welcome guests and invite them to the social hour. All members are encouraged to seek out and speak to all guests before and after the services, during the passing of the peace, and at the social hour.

CULTIVATION/RECRUITMENT

A cultivation team member gets the names of first-time visitors from the friendship folders and phones those people Sunday afternoon or evening, welcoming them and inviting them back. Then the pastor should receive a list of guests on Monday and send letters of welcome to them.

A card with the guests' names, addresses, and phone numbers are sent to "apostles" (cultivators/recruiters) to follow up the pastor's letter with a phone call later in the week so there are three contacts in the first week. The apostles follow up with these persons monthly and offer to meet them at church, answer questions, and invite them to some activity (without being pushy).

When guests begin thinking about membership, a pastor or apostle can arrange a visit. The cultivators/recruiters (apostles) meet monthly with a staff person to share the responses of guests contacted.

INQUIRY/ORIENTATION SESSIONS

Hold inquiry/orientation sessions monthly or as often as needed. Hear from all prospective members as much of their background as they choose to share (take notes to include biographical description in the church newsletter if and when they join). Share the following with the guests:

- the biblical nature and mission of the church
- the history and theology of the denomination
- the history and distinguishing characteristics of the church (preferably with videotapes or PowerPoint visual presentations)
- the church's expectations of membership (i.e., regular worship; everyone participates in a discipling, spiritual growth group

every year; everyone participates in one ministry of the church every year according to one's biblical spiritual gifts; everyone becomes a tither or tither-in process)

- the ministries of the church, from which each is expected to choose one ministry in which to work
- the spiritual gift inventory, which each person fills out to discern his/her spiritual gifts
- an estimate-of-giving card
- a tour of the buildings
- procedures for receiving new members within a worship service

ASSIMILATION

It is critical to help new members feel that they truly "belong" to the church family. To aid in assimilation, provide name tags to new members. Provide them with sponsors or "first friends," who will aid them in making six new friends in the church within six months and will help them become involved in the church.

Write biographical sketches of the new members for the church newsletter. Post pictures of the new members on a prominent bulletin board. Have members of the ministries chosen by the new members contact them, invite them to participate, and get them involved. Have special meals several times a year for new members to meet and make friends.

INACTIVE MEMBER MINISTRY

To encourage formerly active members to become involved again, the pastor could send handwritten "I miss you" notes to people absent for one month. Two assimilation team members should request a visit with those who have been absent for two to three months to listen, seek to understand any problems, and see if they are having any personal crises. You might use trained Stephen Ministers for this. Some of these inactives might be referred to the staff, depending on what the problems might be.

Follow up these steps by contacting inactive members who have been gone one year or more about their desires regarding membership.

Organizing Evangelism Ministry Teams

How do we go about organizing an evangelism ministry that is open to all who have the biblical spiritual gifts of evangelism and hospitality? What is there to do for all those people? Keep in mind that we are *not* organizing a "committee" whose task is to come together monthly to set policy and then go home and forget about it for a month before reassembling to hear the minutes of what was done at the last meeting, listen to a treasurer's report, and then set more policy. Instead, we are organizing a group of gifted, actively involved persons whose task is to do the ministry of evangelism in the church with the coaching, teaching, and training of the staff.

What is working within mainline Protestant churches is the formation of a number of ministerial teams within the evangelism ministry, again based on the spiritual gifts of the participants. The basic tasks/ministries of each of the eight ministry teams delineated below are as follows:

a. develop a year-long plan for "doing its ministry" within the context of the church's five-year plan

b. develop the goals for the evangelism ministry team (what needs to be achieved) and corresponding strategies (how you will accomplish your goals)

c. spend most of your time and efforts at "doing" (executing) your ministry rather than attending meetings

d. meet only as you need in order to set goals and strategies and accomplish them (some of your gatherings may include all members; others might include two or three over the phone or at lunch working on a particular task)

e. determine a leader and a coach of each team, who will meet quarterly with the leaders and coaches of the other teams to review what is happening in all the ministry teams, evaluate and possibly recommend new strategies, as well as plan the overall evangelism goals, strategies, and budget for the subsequent year

"Every Member Evangelism" Training Team

Basic tasks/ministries:

a. Educate the members/youth/children of the congregation in the biblical-theological understandings of evangelism; and b) educate and train members/youth/children in "every member evangelism" (how to "bubble enthusiastically" regarding life in the Spirit of Jesus to each person's network of two hundred-plus people each already knows).

Servant Evangelism Team

Basic Task/Ministry:

Engage in a "ministry of unconditional love" by performing "random acts of kindness with no strings attached" for the people of your church's service area (a twenty minute drive by car in all directions).

Publicity Ministry Team

Basic task/ministry:

Proclaim the "good news" of life in Christ Jesus as it is being experienced in the life of your church to your church's service area in creative, multiple ways.

Hospitality Ministry Team

Basic task/ministry:

Provide Christian hospitality to all who enter the doors of your church and educate/train the congregation to do the same.

CULTIVATION/RECRUITMENT MINISTRY (APOSTLES)

Basic task/ministry:

Follow up with visitors/guests who attend your church with a warm welcome, friendship, information, introductions to others, and invitations to return and participate in the life of the church.

INQUIRY/ORIENTATION MINISTRY

Basic task/ministry:

Provide creative, effective inquiry/orientation sessions as needed for prospective members and those desiring more information.

ASSIMILATION MINISTRY

Basic task/ministry:

Develop and execute a comprehensive plan for helping to assimilate new members into the life of the congregation.

INACTIVE MEMBER MINISTRY

Basic task/ministry:

Develop and execute a plan to contact, listen to, understand, and care for members who become inactive (as outlined in the precceding section).

This type of team approach staffed by one or more persons on each ministry team can accommodate any number of participants in the evangelism ministry. It also frees people up to do ministry according to their spiritual gifts rather than attending typical monthly "committee" meetings in which all members are expected to work together on most everything, thereby accomplishing little.

chapter nine

Worship

LIVING CHURCHES

Worship is designed to reach and connect with the unchurched (never been to church) and the dechurched (once active, no longer), as well as the current members. Thus, both traditional and contemporary worship services are offered.

Worship uses the language, music, and technology of the people who it is trying to reach (the 50 to 60 percent unchurched/dechurched of our time), as well as that of the current members.

Worship is Holy Spirit-filled!

Worship is planned by a worship team (pastor and the directors of music, drama, and visuals).

DYING CHURCHES

Worship is designed to connect with the current members; only traditional worship is offered.

Worship uses the language, music, and technology of the current members (mainly those over fifty-five years old).

Worship is often Holy Spirit-less, mainly going through the motions, forms, and rituals.

Worship is planned by the pastor with musical offerings supplied by the music staff.

Worship planning for contemporary services begins with contemporary life situations, then reaches back to the Bible for guidance and answers. Planning for traditional services begins with prescribed lectionary verse and seeks to make them relevant.	All worship planning begins with prescribed lectionary Bible verses, then attempts to make them meaningful.

Why Changes are Necessary in Worship

In the ministry of worship we must distinguish between substance and form. The substance of Christian worship in every age and culture remains the same—it is the Gospel, the "good news of life in Christ Jesus and in the realm of God on earth," which Jesus proclaimed was present and into which he invited all to participate.

However, the forms for communicating this good news (the substance) *always has changed and must continue to change* if we are to reach people of every age and time. Moreover, we must attempt to reach all of the people in every age group—for that was Jesus' command to all his followers in his own time and thereafter: "Go therefore and make disciples of all nations . . ." (Matt. 28:19). Jesus did not say, "Go and bring into God's kingdom a select few who appreciate the same worship forms of language and music that you do"!

The forms of worship in the first-century churches were very simple and much different from our traditional worship of today. In Acts 2:42–47 we read:

> They devoted themselves to the apostles' teaching and fellowship, to the breaking of bread and the prayers. Awe came upon everyone, because many wonders and signs were being done by the apostles. All who believed were together and had all things in common;

they would sell their possessions and goods and distribute the proceeds to all, as they had need. Day by day, as they spent much time together in the temple, they broke bread at home and ate their food with glad and generous hearts, praising God and having the goodwill of all the people. And day by day the Lord added to their number those who were being saved.

Thus, we see a very informal, simple type of worship centered in daily worship at the Jewish temple simultaneously interwoven with a close fellowship in their homes involving eating together (even as they did with Jesus), learning from the apostles, prayer and joyful praise of God, proclaiming the good news of life in Christ Jesus with as many as they could reach, and sharing all they had with each other and the hurting within the larger community—and growing in number day by day!

How different this worship life was from the forms it took after 300 C.E. when the Roman Emperor Constantine declared that all of his subjects would henceforth be Christian and would worship as the priests of the time decided, leading to the centrality of the Mass recited in Latin, chanting (in Latin) between the priests and choirs, robes, incense, crucifixes, statues of saints, and all the trappings that Christendom took on.

Then, in 1517, Martin Luther came to the conclusion that the traditional forms of worship needed to be changed since they were no longer communicating or connecting with the German people. He felt strongly that the substance of the faith needed to be communicated through the language, music, and technology of the people whom the church was trying to reach. Thus, he wanted to use the German language rather than Latin in order to reach his people, and risked his life to do so, hiding out in the Wartburg Castle for more than a year translating the Bible into German. He went to the "biergartens" of Germany to hear the types of music to which the people were listening and appreciating, and he began writing hymns in German that they could sing themselves rather than listening to the priests and choirs chant in Latin. Moreover, he wanted to make use of the new technological invention of his time, the printing press, so that the German people could read and sing from their own Bibles and hymnals. And for daring to change the traditional forms of worship of his time, as well as the theology, he was persecuted, put on trial, pronounced guilty, excommunicated, and had to hide from the religious establishment.

John and Charles Wesley similarly changed the forms of worship used by the Church of England when they "borrowed" the musical ballads of the common people of England for their many beloved hymns. Indeed, the church throughout history has always been the most vital when it communicated the substance of the faith, the good news of life in Christ Jesus and in God's earthly realm, in the language, music, and technology of the people whom it was trying to reach.

Now today, the once new worship forms created by Luther, the Wesleys, and other Protestant reformers have become the traditional worship of our time. From 1517 to the present, the worship forms used in Europe and America have remained fairly constant, characterized mainly by European hymns and classical music, organs, choirs, robes, stoles, printed Bibles, hymnals and bulletins, liturgy from Books of Worship, creeds, oratorical sermons appealing primarily to the mind, stained glass windows, and an atmosphere of formality and stateliness. In other words, the once new language, music, and technology that was needed to communicate with the people of one hundred to five hundred years ago has today become the traditional language, music, and technology that is hindering and stopping the church from reaching the majority of people in the United States (as well as in Canada and Europe).

The language, music, and technology of traditional worship in mainline Protestant churches today is not contemporary for the post-1946 generations. Imagine that an unchurched person, who has never stepped foot into a church, finally decides to come and find out what it is like. Once there, he/she reads words in the bulletin and is invited to participate in things called Prelude, Introit, Collect, Gloria Patri, Doxology, Sanctus, and Postlude! This person wonders, "What foreign country have I entered?" Moreover, he/she is asked to sing the Gloria Patri and Doxology without any words being printed in the bulletin.

Oh, there may have been a page number for the Gloria Patri and Doxology, but by the time the newcomer turns to the correct pages, the songs are over! Then the newcomer is asked to say "The Lord's Prayer" and use "debts" or "trespasses," and again, he/she doesn't have the slightest idea what "The Lord's Prayer" is, and no words are printed in the bulletin! It is clear that we design our worship for the current members who already know what all these strange-sounding things are and how to participate! This also clearly reveals that we really don't want the unchurched to worship with us, unless of course they are willing to stick around long enough to learn what we do and how we do it, and then are willing to do it our way! But most post-1946 generations are showing us that they aren't willing to stick around long enough to do it our way, because we aren't communicating with them in their language.

Nor are we connecting with them with their music any more than the Roman Catholic Church's Gregorian chants in Latin were communicating with the German people in 1517. What percentage of people in the United States today purchase CDs of organ music, traditional hymnody, or even classical music? Not more than 5 percent of our population purchases CDs of all three of these forms of music put together! Yet, these are the primary forms of music we use in our worship services! Are we going to be content to reach only 5 percent of the people around us? Are we even trying to communicate and connect with the post-1946 generations in our society, most of whom have either left the church or have never set foot into it unless for a wedding or funeral?!

Didn't Jesus say, "Go to all people everywhere and make them my disciples?" Oh, I have heard some traditionally oriented church music directors say, "Someday these younger people will grow up and appreciate 'good' music once again!" or "The pendulum always swings back and forth, and it will again!" The problem is that the pendulum hasn't swung back since 1965, and all indications are that it's not coming back, even as it did not swing back in Luther's time! Yes, there are handsful of younger people who are into meditation today and appreciating classical music, but thousands of the younger generations are flocking to the churches that use upbeat, spirit-filled, heart-centered Christian music written in the last thirty years!

Nor are we using the technologies of today in our worship services—television, videos, DVDs, screens, CDs, computers, excellent sound systems, dramatic lighting, multimedia, synthesizers, and electric guitars. Traditional worship has been and continues to use primarily the technology of five hundred years ago: pianos and organs, the printing press to print bulletins, hymnals, and Bibles. The pre-1946 generations, including my own, were raised with the radio, wind-up record players, and black-and-white movies. But the post-1946 generations have been brought up on television, videos, computers, DVDs, CDs, and electronic instruments. They watched screens, while we primarily listened and read. Even as the Protestant reformers felt the need to use the technology of their time to reach the European people in the 1500s, so we today must use the technologies of our time to communicate the Christian faith to the people of today.

Resistance to Change Leads to Decline

What we are discovering today is that the churches that have used solely traditional worship forms from the past five hundred years (with a few exceptions) are plateaued or declining in worship attendance and membership, because this type of service communicates mainly with those born before 1946 (other than those boomers who were brought up in and stayed in the church). However, the great majority of baby boomers (born 1946 to 1964) and generation X (born 1965 to-1983) have been turned off and do not attend these services today. For instance, the United Church of Christ has lost more than 700,000, over one-third, of its membership since 1965, and other mainline denominations are experiencing similar declines with no end in sight to the downward spirals. As indicated in chapter 1, a Christian research firm, empty tomb, inc.[1], predicts that unless mainline Protestant churches make some major changes in what they currently are doing, most of these churches will be gone as early as 2032—only decades away!

On the other hand, most churches that are growing today use a minimum of 30 percent contemporary music (composed since 1970) in their worship services, as well as incorporating more modern instruments (electronic keyboards, guitars, drums), drama, and visuals. Moreover, the churches that are growing the most rapidly design different worship services to reach the different generations—a more traditional or blended traditional/contemporary form of worship for the generation born before 1946 (which also communicates with some dechurched baby boomers); a celebration/praise service for the boomers; and multimedia, fast-paced, tuned-up, loud, interactive service for generation X. The fastest growing churches (e.g., the Church of Joy (ELCA), Glendale, Arizona) even have different services for older and younger boomers, as well as for seekers and believers.

Organizing a Ministry of Worship/Spiritual Life

The first step in making worship more relevant for today is to develop a ministry of worship/spiritual life as opposed to a committee or board of worship. Rather than having a nominating committee nominate and the congregation elect two to three persons each year for three-year terms on a worship committee or board, after which they must leave that committee or board and be elected to another (for which they may or may not be gifted), give all members of the church a spiritual gift inventory to help them discern their biblical spiritual gifts. Then have the spiritual gift ministry team encourage and invite those members who have the spiritual gifts of apostleship, prophecy, teaching, encouragement, knowledge, faith, discernment, and interpretation—all those who have a passion for helping others to know God as revealed in Jesus Christ and to increasingly live according to God's way to participate in the ministry of worship and spiritual growth.

These people do not come together once a month for a meeting to set policy, but instead they do ministry by working on ministry teams according to their gifts and passions. Each will serve on one or more teams, such as a choir, praise team, praise band, gen X band, chancel art, communion, drama, visuals, sound, lighting, computers, Bible studies, and prayer groups. The leaders or coaches of these teams might meet quarterly or be on call as needed to help coordinate the whole effort with the staff. These teams also set policy as needed along with their coaches/staff. Moreover, those on the ministry teams do not need to stop doing what they are doing after a two- to three-year term. They decide each year whether they will continue or not, and they may continue doing this ministry for as long as they have the spiritual gifts and passion for it.

Developing Different Types of Worship Services

Traditional Worship

This service is meaningful mainly to those born prior to 1946, although some younger people find it meets their needs as well (especially those brought up in the church and who never left it). It will be necessary to keep a form of traditional worship for another twenty to thirty years, as it communicates and connects with those who have been stalwarts of our faith over a long period of time—and they deserve to have their needs met for as long as they live!

Significant efforts must be made to keep these services Holy Spirit–filled to avoid just going through motions and ritual. Organists must play the hymns in the spirit in which they were written. All hymns are not meant to be slow and quiet. Choirs must be well-rehearsed. Sermons must be well-prepared and delivered with the necessary passion called for by the topic. Worship forms must communicate with the whole of a person, the heart as well as the head. Words to all responses and the "Lord's Prayer" should be printed so unchurched persons attending will be able to participate.

Traditional worship is best held in a beautiful, well-kept sanctuary. (However, remember that churches that use only this form of worship have been declining since 1965 and are projected to continue to do so, with most being gone within another thirty-plus years.)

BLENDED TRADITIONAL/CONTEMPORARY WORSHIP

This service communicates with those born prior to 1946, as well as some boomers (born 1946 to 1964) and a few generation X (born 1965 to 1983) especially those who have remained in the church, but it will not attract too many unchurched (never been to church) since it is considered too "churchy" and "foreign" to their experience.

This service should utilize at least 30 percent contemporary music (written in the last thirty years). Note: Old hymn tunes that are given contemporary words do not count as contemporary music! We are seeing more of this in new denominational hymnals as a way of contemporizing their hymnals. But it's the traditional hymn tunes, indeed, the hymn form itself, that turns off the younger generations to traditional hymns, as well as the words. The contemporized hymn tunes still don't connect with the younger generations! Moreover, the new denominational hymnals that are trying to contemporize the old hymns in this way are striking out on both ends. The younger generations are turned off by the old hymn tunes, and the older generations are turned off because they now have to sing new words to the old hymns that they have memorized and loved as they were!

See appendix 1 of this book for a sample of this type of service.

CONTEMPORARY BOOMER WORSHIP

This service is designed to connect/communicate with unchurched and dechurched folk who were born between 1946 and 1964. It will also be appealing to some born before 1946 and to some of generation X (born after 1965).

Worship that appeals to baby boomers includes the following:

- relevant messages that focus on how Christian faith applies to and makes a difference in their daily lives (Boomers are spiritually hungry!)
- meaning and values (Boomers are highly confused about these. Do they want their children to do what they did?)

- excellence, quality, expertise in all things—not mediocrity or worse!
- rock and roll, upbeat gospel, celebrative, emotional, "feeling" music!
- a good sound system (it's been part of their lives)
- excitement, action up front—nothing boring!
- good timing in worship (ala TV—no dead spots or awkward transitions)
- new packaging (not the same old thing in the same old way)
- benefits from worship (Boomers want their needs met)
- choices in worship times, types, and music
- friendliness, a sense of belonging, user-friendly worship, easy to get in and be accepted
- a new, clean, well-run, safe nursery for their children
- a full life right now (they are not concerned about the after-life.)

Boomers are looking for a completely contemporary worship experience—one that is of the highest quality, one that focuses on life as they live it today, and one that reveals to them the difference it makes if they accept and live in the way of Jesus as opposed to the ways of the world. They want to be around people who themselves have found the spiritual secrets of living life "abundantly," as Jesus promised.

But they want their worship experiences to communicate with them through the multimedia with which they have grown up and which they understand—music, drama, visuals, sound, and lighting.

Thus, this type of worship is characterized by their kind of music composed in the last thirty years (rock and roll, country, upbeat gospel, celebrative, emotional, "feeling" music), sung by excellent soloists and small groups (who sing with their eyes, smiles, and bodies—not just with their mouths looking down at the words they are singing). Moreover, boomer music is accompanied by their instruments (electronic keyboards, electric guitars, and drums) amplified over excellent sound systems with simultaneous visuals and dance (ala MTV). Humorous drama lifting up contemporary life situations that are addressed later on in the service by a brief scripture reading and message also speak effectively to unchurched and dechurched boomers.

Other elements of this type of service can include the following:

- a series of praise songs sung one after another with repetition of some lines
- a very brief printed liturgy: the music serves as the liturgy, providing the transitions between parts of the worship
- words of songs, brief scripture, and announcements projected on a large screen, often effectively accompanied by appropriate contemporary secular and Christian music
- good, dramatic flow/timing (no breaks more than five seconds when nothing happens)
- an offering, but guests told that they are not expected to contribute as the members take care of that (perhaps with a statement of how much the members have given thus far that year)
- no altar, communion table, or other Christian symbols (with which the unchurched are unfamiliar and dechurched are uncomfortable)
- no gowns, robes, or stoles
- excellence/quality in all that happens within the service.

This service is best held in a large, clean, well-kept auditorium, with few or no Christian symbols. Some church sanctuaries may work if the permanent symbols are contemporary in nature, and the front of the sanctuary is a large, flexible space to allow drama, dance, and several musical groups to function simultaneously. A large, permanent screen is required for visuals. Rear view projection is best for a sanctuary that has too much daylight. An excellent sound system and lighting are also required for a quality service.

A plan for creating a service of this type and a sample are provided in appendix 2 of this book.

Contemporary Worship for Generation X
(born 1965 to 1983)

This service, again, is aimed at reaching unchurched and de-churched young people of this generation with their language, music, technology, thought patterns, and issues and concerns as they grow into maturity. Most folks born before 1946 will not appreciate this type of worship, but then, gen Xers don't appreciate traditional forms of worship either. That's why they are not coming to traditional services.

Worship that appeals to generation X includes the following:

- relevant messages pertaining to this generation's current life situations that reveal how Christian faith makes life more authentic and real (Gen Xers are spiritually hungry for authenticity in life and are exploring many religions and philosophies for answers to their deepest questions.)
- messages communicated through stories, testimonies, sound bites, visuals, and deep sharing among their peers—as opposed to oratory or lectures
- their music—loud, hard rock, emotional, "real/authentic" music composed since 1980, as well as some secular music that has deep, authentic meanings to them
- their instruments played loudly by their people—acoustical guitars, drums, keyboard
- computer-driven multimedia, multivisual, multisensory experiences (ala MTV)
- a very casual, come-as-you-are atmosphere. (They want to be accepted as they are.)
- discussions within worship to share with each other regarding certain issues raised in the very brief scripture, message, testimonies, and multimedia presentations (Best to have folk sit around round tables with some nibble food and drinks.)

- small group opportunities available following worship to interact, study the faith, pray, serve others, and get their lives sorted out and manageable
- something "happening" to them during each service (They want to have a meaningful "experience" that matters.)

This service cannot be held in a sanctuary with permanent pews. It is best held in a fellowship hall or auditorium not filled with traditional symbols. The room needs a feeling of intimacy with round tables and chairs for discussions and sharing—and don't forget the food!

The service is planned by the pastor/staff person, and the music, drama, and visuals directors. Effective visuals often include interviews with other gen Xers to lift up topics for discussions around the tables.

There is a sample of this type of service in appendix 3 of this book.

chapter ten

Stewardship

Living Churches

In stewardship, the mission is to develop faithful stewards of God's overwhelming, unfailing abundance.

A comprehensive, year-round ministry of stewardship is developed that includes stewardship education of the congregation, annual stewardship spiritual growth events (campaigns), a spiritual gift ministry to help all to discern their spiritual gifts and to participate in one ministry of the church every year, and a continuing ministry gifts program (a church endowment fund).

All members are expected, encouraged, and helped to become tithers or tithers-in-process as a "spiritual discipline" to help them become givers more like God.

Dying Churches

The mission is to raise enough money to pay the bills, preferably from nonmembers via fundraisers.

Organize a periodic committee to raise the necessary monies for the next year.

Tithing is never mentioned so as not to scare members.

All members are expected to participate in one ministry of the church each year based on their spiritual gifts and may continue working in that ministry as long as they have the gifts and passion for it.	A few are nominated and elected each year to staff the church's committees for two- to three-year terms, after which they must leave that committee and be elected to another (for which they may or may not be gifted).
A continuing ministry gifts program (church endowment fund) enables the congregation to be faithful stewards of their accumulated assets.	The church does not have or want a church endowment fund so as to not hurt annual giving.

Basis in Biblical Understandings of Stewardship

Living churches base the entirety of their stewardship ministry on God's teachings as revealed in our Bibles, as opposed to dying churches that base their understandings of stewardship on the teachings of this world—the two of which are opposite of each other! Here in brief form are the major biblical understandings of stewardship.

God has given each of us existence in an abundant, overflowing universe, giving us everything we are and have—life, health, eyesight, hearing, strength, sun, moon, mountains, trees, birds, animals, families, friends, hugs and held hands, abilities, interests, work, money, food, clothing, shelter, possessions, luxuries, and God's steadfast love, forgiveness, presence, and power at all times and places (Gen. 1, 2; Matt. 6: 25–34; John 10:10; Isa. 43:1–2).

Becoming aware of the overflowing abundance God showers upon us, we are a grateful people at all times and in all circumstances, knowing that God's blessings in every moment exceed our temporary problems (1 Thess. 5:16–18; Phil. 4:6, 11–13).

We do not own anything to do with as we please, but we are God's stewards, caretakers, of all the households (*oikos*) God has given us to manage: our personal lives (bodies, minds, spirits, relationships); our families and homes; our work and workplaces; our churches; our communities, nations, and wider world; our global environment; and our accumulated assets after death (Gen. 1:26–31, 2:15; Luke 12:13–21; 2 Cor. 8:13–15).

We are created "in the image of God" with the potential to be like God, to become givers like God! Indeed, to become all that we are meant to be, we must develop a giving spirit, a giving attitude, in all areas of life (Gen. 1:26–27; Luke 6:38; 2 Corinthians 8:9, 9:6–11).

Thus, giving is not a burden, but an opportunity to grow spiritually by becoming increasingly like God, to further God's purposes in this world, to share God's values and way with others, to help all God's children now and in the future, to participate in the abundant flow of the universe, not out of guilt, fear, or greed, but toward the ends of joy, satisfaction, fulfillment, love, and spiritual growth (2 Cor. 8:1–5, 9:7–14).

And when we give, we discover that the more we give, the more we receive of all kinds of God's wondrous blessings. We cannot outgive our good God (Prov. 3:9–10, 11:24–25; Mal. 3:10; Luke 6:38; Mark 10:28–30; 2 Cor. 9:6).

The Role of the Pastor/Staff Person/Coach

The person providing staff leadership for this ministry must have the spiritual gifts and passion for it because he/she must be a teacher, preacher, and an example of the biblical theology of stewardship. He/she must be one who has developed a God-like giving attitude and spirit, resulting in being an eager, joyful giver!

This person preaches stewardship sermons, teaches classes, writes newsletter articles, provides resources, and accompanies other stewardship leaders to continuing stewardship education events. He/she aids the stewardship ministry members in developing a vision, goals, long-term and annual strategies, and annual budgets, and in preparing annual evaluations and planning. This person also makes calls on certain members (leaders and those with the most potential for giving) for annual and capital campaigns, as well as for continuing ministry gifts for the church endowment fund.

This staff leader also must be allowed to know what the church members give so they can help create different, effective approaches to be used for congregational members who are at different levels of growth in giving, and for receiving feedback on the spiritual growth of the members of the flock. Even as parents use different approaches when their child is learning to walk, so the pastor or stewardship staff person needs to develop different ways to communicate with members of the congregation who are at different stages in learning to give joyfully and eagerly.

Good parents do not spank a child who is just learning to walk. Instead, they take the child by the arms and lovingly help them take the next step. On the other hand, the toddler who is now walking, albeit unsteadily, needs another form of help from the parents, and the child who is leaping and dancing receives a whole different type of encouragement from the parents!

Similarly, the stewardship staff person needs to help design different approaches for the different people in the congregation, depending on their growth in the giving spirit. If they are just learning to walk in stewardship, they need one approach (perhaps, a suggestion of moving up one giving step of one hundred to two hundred dollars per year). Those who are walking, but not yet jumping and dancing in stewardship, need another approach (perhaps a suggestion to move up an additional 1 percent of their household income in the next year). And for those who are already leaping and dancing in stewardship, it might be recommended that they go for the full tithe and beyond!

Now in our churches, when no one but the financial secretary knows how much church members give, we must send the same stewardship letter to all members, thereby missing most everyone. Living churches have broken the "conspiracy of silence" about money in the church. Dying churches trust only the financial secretary, even more than the pastor. Living churches know that Jesus spoke about money and/or possessions 30 percent of the time. Count his sayings in the four Gospels. Of Jesus' thirty-nine teaching parables, twenty-one were about money and/or possessions. Moreover, in the church in the first century, there was no "conspiracy of silence" regarding money and/or possessions either. Check out the story of Ananias and Sapphira in Acts 5:1–11.

Why do we have this silence about money in our churches? I suggest it is because there are three things our culture has told us we must not talk about with people we know—religion, politics, and money! And we have been obeying our culture with a passion in these three areas. But is our culture the god we obey, or is God/Jesus the ruler of our lives and of the church? If we may not speak about religion with those we know, we cannot do the ministry of evangelism. If we may not speak about politics, then we cannot do the ministry of Christian witness in society. And, if we may not speak about money and possessions, then we cannot do the ministry of stewardship. Is it any wonder that these three major ministries of the church have been the most neglected and least effective ministries of mainline Protestant churches over the last fifty-plus years?

Thus, the conspiracy of silence about money in the church today is one of the major factors that is "killing" the church in our time, because it hinders—indeed stops—effective stewardship ministry in the church, and most churches today do not have either the financial or people resources they need to continue to function.

The pastor/stewardship staff person also needs to know how much people in the church give in order to receive feedback regarding the spiritual growth of members of the congregation. And we have seen that giving money is a sign of spiritual growth. If we want to keep our pastor in the dark regarding our spiritual growth, let's also make our pastor wear a blindfold when he/she leads weekly worship so he/she cannot know who attends worship or not! I know that some laity say that if the pastor knows what they give (especially if they don't give very much), then the pastor won't provide pastoral care when it is needed. My response is "We pastors (like Jesus) spend most of our time with sinners!" Still other laity fear that the pastor won't keep their financial giving confidential. My response is, "Do you trust your financial secretary more than you trust your pastor? Of course we trust our financial secretaries, but we also can and need to trust our pastors!

Indeed, pastors keep all kinds of other items confidential, and any pastor worth his/her salt will also keep individual financial giving in confidence.

Participants in the Ministry of Stewardship

Do not have a nominating nommittee find people who are breathing and who will say "yes" to serve on a stewardship nommittee or board that comes together in September to begin wondering what to do for a November campaign to raise the necessary funds for the following year. That is what dying churches do, and that's why they are dying! Don't put a person on the ministry of stewardship who complains that "the church is always asking for money." That's like putting a fox in a chicken coop! If you want to kill your ministry of stewardship, allow that person to spread their unbiblical poison.

Instead, living churches invite all those in the church who have the biblical spiritual gifts of stewardship (giving, encouragement, faith) and have a passion for this ministry, those who are tithers or tithers-in-process, those who are aware of their abundance, are grateful, and are eager to give of themselves and what they have of their money, time, effort, and abilities to this most important work of God.

Invite these persons to make stewardship their primary ministry in the church over the next two or three years, and if they wish to continue after that, they may for as long as they have the biblical gifts and passion for it! Moreover, each year keep inviting more people with these gifts into the ministry so that it continues to grow and expand its work.

What do you do with all these people? Each serves on one of several stewardship teams, again depending on individual gifts and interests (see the following section). These "teams" could consist of one, two, three, or more persons depending on the task at hand and/or the number of people with whom they have to work. Moreover, all of these people are not required to attend a monthly stewardship ministry meeting (praise God!). Only the leaders of each team would meet quarterly to report, strategize, evaluate, and plan. The goal is to free our hard-working, busy people from attending monthly "reporting" meetings, so they can spend their time doing ministry within their teams. They would connect with each other over the phone, at lunch, in the church parlor on Sunday mornings, or wherever and whenever they decide it is necessary to do their work. The most important thing is to *accomplish the mission* rather than attending meetings!

Stewardship Education Team

The mission of the stewardship education team is to increasingly develop faithful stewards of God's overwhelming and unfailing abundance among the adults, youth, and children of the congregation. To accomplish this task it would seek to educate the congregation—inundate the minds and hearts of their people with the biblical understandings of being stewards as delineated earlier in this chapter (see also appendix 4, "Scripture Passages on Stewardship").

The team should encourage the pastor(s) to preach a number of stewardship sermons every year, rather than just one on Stewardship Sunday. (There are numerous sermon topics to be drawn from the biblical basis of stewardship discussed earlier in this chapter.) Insert stewardship "one-liners" in the Sunday bulletins, such as "You cannot outgive God," "Give, and it will be given to you" (Luke 6:38), and "God loves a cheerful giver" (2 Cor. 9:7). See "Stewardship One-Liners" in appendix 5 for more suggestions. Use stewardship quotations both in the Sunday bulletins and newsletters, such as "A nongiving Christian is a contradiction in terms" and "Our unprecedented wealth and prosperity, unchecked and ill-managed, has led us to a poverty of soul." Both these quotes are from the great stewardship book by Donald Hinze, *To Give and Give Again*.[1]

The stewardship education team should have a stewardship page in each church newsletter; stewardship classes need to be developed for adults; and youth ministries need to have some sessions every year on Christian stewardship, for example, "What are you going to do with what you have been given?" In addition, entire curricula have been developed on stewardship for children (for more information, contact the Union Church of Hinsdale, Hinsdale, Illinois[2]).

Banners, posters, videos, and drama are also helpful media for communicating the biblical understandings of being God's managers (stewards) of the abundance we have been given by our good, gracious God.

Annual Stewardship Spiritual Growth Event Team

Instead of calling this a "stewardship campaign," which leads people to think of it as the annual money-raising campaign when they have to pledge their money and talent to the church, I like to refer to it as the "Stewardship Spiritual Growth Event." Each member has the opportunity to grow spiritually by becoming more like God as we develop a more giving attitude and spirit. This is made possible by our becoming more aware of our abundance, more grateful for all we have been given, and, correspondingly, more eager to give more substantially and joyfully than ever before!

The Stewardship Spiritual Growth Event team has the responsibility of planning and executing this event. The most important thing they need to do every time they gather is to *engage in Bible study and prayer* using the plethora of stewardship passages in the Bible (see a partial list of these in appendix 4), because unless the stewardship ministry folk are imbued with and focused on the biblical understandings of being stewards, they will never be able to assist the congregation to grow in the "image" of our ever-giving God.

The planning needs to begin immediately following the preceding year's event, usually in January or February (if the event occurred the preceding November with the follow-up and results being fully known by January). The first step in planning for the next event is to conduct a thorough evaluation of the preceding year's event. What were the results in terms of the spiritual stewardship growth of our people, as well as the levels of participation of our people in the ministries of the church and the money that was pledged? What was effective? What did not work so well? What do we need to do to improve?

The next steps are to develop the theme, the basic type of event (see the various types and effectiveness of them below), and the various methodologies that will be used to accomplish our mission of continued spiritual growth of our people in being God's faithful stewards. Then, specific persons and groups would be given responsibility for developing the various tasks that need to be accomplished—creating materials (publicity, stewardship education, flip charts, videos, letters to the congregation, pledge cards, spiritual gift inventory questionnaires, thank you notes, etc.), inviting speakers, planning meals, and the myriad of other tasks that are necessary.

There is so much that needs to be done (to do it well) and that is why we must begin in January or February for the November event. "To fail to plan, is to plan to fail!"

The churches that begin in September to begin thinking how they are going to raise the necessary money for the next year, send out the same letter to everyone with a pledge card, and just take what happens to be returned with no follow-up are dying churches! These churches deserve to die, because they are doing all the right things to assure an early death.

GOALS OF EFFECTIVE STEWARDSHIP SPIRITUAL GROWTH EVENTS

The first and most important goal of an effective Stewardship Spiritual Growth Event is to teach biblical stewardship within each of these annual events. Teach people that "Every important decision we make in life is a stewardship decision!" Since God has given us everything that we are and have, God is the "owner" of all we are and have. We are but God's stewards, caretakers, managers (on behalf of and in obedience to God) of our personal lives, families and homes, work and workplaces, churches, communities, states/nations, global environment, and our accumulated assets after we die.

Thus, the most important decisions in life are stewardship decisions: What am I going to do with what God has given me? Am I going to go to finish high school, go to college or vocational school, or get a job? Am I going to get married? How many children will we have? What job will I take? Where will we live? Will we rent an apartment or buy a home? Will we get a new car this year or next and what type of car? When will I retire? What will I do in my retirement? How will I plan for my death? Will I donate my organs to others? What will I do with my accumulated assets?

Every important decision in life is a stewardship decision! What will I do with what I have been given by God? (That includes everything I am and have!)

Thus, the primary purpose of teaching biblical stewardship in every annual Stewardship Spiritual Growth Event is to *change our peoples' thinking* from self-centered/worldly perspectives to God-centered ones. We are in the business of transforming lives rather than just raising money, although the money will be there when lives are transformed.

A second biblically based goal is to help people understand that they are "made in the image of God," which means they have the potential and are capable of being more like God as they increasingly become more giving persons by allowing the living Spirit of God/Jesus to come into and transform their hearts and minds. Since God was and is the "Great Giver," we need to help each member increasingly develop a more giving spirit, a more giving attitude, and thereby become increasingly more like God. Again, rather than primarily seeking to raise money, we are instead in the process of helping our people grow spiritually, to be more like our great, giving God!

So, let us *not* ask our people to give to help us pay our bills! Do *not* ask people to give to support our church's budget! No one gets excited about paying bills or supporting budgets! That is too little to ask! Instead, let us ask our people to *give to become givers more like God!* Let us ask our people to give because each of us has a need to give to be fully human!

A third goal of an effective Stewardship Spiritual Growth Event is to encourage people to use the tithe as a spiritual discipline to enable them to become the givers God intends them to be. The biblical tithe is not a law that all must follow. But it is a most helpful spiritual discipline to aid folks in growing to be more giving, and thereby becoming more like God. As they move toward the tithe, they gradually discover the eternal truth that God provides, and that they need to rely on God for what they have. They gradually become more eager to give substantially and proportionately. They gradually experience the biblical truth that the more you give, the more you receive in life of all kinds of God's wondrous blessings—that you cannot outgive God!

It has been found helpful in a number of living churches to provide some tithing goals to help people grow toward the tithe, for example, 3 percent as an immediate goal, 5 percent as a growth goal, and 10 percent as an ultimate goal.

A fourth goal of an effective Stewardship Spiritual Growth Event is to aid followers of Jesus in discerning their biblical spiritual gifts and to use them in ministry within Christ's church as the Apostle Paul recommended to the early churches in Corinth, Ephesus, and Rome (1 Cor. 12:4–11, 27–31; Eph. 4:11–12; Rom. 12:4–9). (See chapter 6, "Church Organization" for a full delineation of this concept and how it works.)

I know that a number of living churches use different times of the year for receiving monetary pledges and obtaining commitments to work in the ministries of the church according to the spiritual gifts of their people, while still others seek both at the same time. It works either way if they use biblical understandings of being faithful stewards of money and spiritual gifts, develop creative methods, and are willing to work hard.

A fifth goal is to provide the necessary people and financial resources to enable the church of Jesus Christ to be what God desires and what it can be. See also appendix 6, "Effective Stewardship Spiritual Growth Events (Campaigns)."

Spiritual Gifts Ministry Team

The mission of the spiritual gifts ministry team is to aid as many members as possible in discerning the biblical spiritual gifts God has given each of them and encouraging and enlisting every member to become involved in one ministry of the church each year according to those gifts. This is done by giving a spiritual gifts inventory to as many members of the congregation as possible throughout the year (including each group of new members who enters during the year), and aiding them in becoming connected with a ministry that corresponds with their spiritual gifts and for which they have a passion. (See appendix 7 of this book for a chart of the biblical spiritual gifts and the ministries of the church that correspond to them.)

Moreover, these persons may continue to work in a ministry for which they have the spiritual gifts for as long as they have those gifts, a sense of "calling" from God to be about this ministry, and a passion for it. Since most people have several spiritual gifts, they may choose to work in any ministry for which they have the gifts, but each is encouraged to spend the most time and energy in one ministry every year.

Continuing Ministry Gifts Team

The mission of the continuing ministry gifts team is to help the people of the church be faithful stewards of their accumulated assets by developing, strengthening, conducting, and coordinating a church endowment fund.

I prefer to call a church endowment fund "continuing ministry gifts," because then we are then using theological rather than banking language. To many people the word "endowment" speaks of banks and finances, whereas "continuing ministry gifts" speaks of helping our people think about continuing their ministry in Christ's church even after they are gone from this world. They love their church and have enjoyed working in it over many years, but most have never thought it was possible, nor did they know how, to continue their ministries through their church after they leave this earth.

I visited one of my laypersons who was a mainstay of our church choir for a long time and said to him, "Russ, you have been singing in our choir for more than fifty years. After you're gone that choir won't be the same without you! You're going to have to keep singing in that choir!" He laughed and asked, "But how I can I do that?" I replied, "If you would leave something in your estate for the music ministry of our church, you will keep singing in that choir!" He died at age ninety-six after singing in the choir for sixty years and left his entire estate to our church (he had no family other than the church and that choir). Fifty percent of his estate was given to the music ministry and 50 percent was given to the church at large!

There are three main reasons why a church should consider having a continuing ministry gifts program (a church endowment fund). The first is that it enables churches to help broaden the understanding of Christian stewardship beyond a "means to raise funds annually for the church" by stressing the biblical understanding of the stewardship of all of life, including and especially being God's faithful, grateful stewards, caretakers, and managers of all that God has enabled us to accumulate during our entire lives.

The second reason why churches should consider having a continuing ministry gifts program is to provide another pastoral service to members, helping them to think through their own personal stewardship of life, relate it to their unique situations, and plan to continue their ministries on behalf of Jesus' realm after they die. It is estimated that one of six families needs help to deal with their accumulated wealth and the necessary financial planning, and the church needs to participate in that part of the financial planning, which refers to that person's faithful stewarding of what they have been given by God throughout their life.

The third reason for churches to consider a continuing ministry gifts program is to provide the extra financial resources needed to expand Christ's ministries through a local church when the opportunities present themselves and the church doesn't have the adequate monies in the operating budget to do it.

I know that there are many clergy and laity within the church who are opposed to churches having endowment funds, based on some experiences with churches that poured such a large percentage of the endowment fund dollars into the operating budgets of churches, only to have the stewardship of its members decrease because they began relying on the endowment to fund the ministries of the church. However, it is possible for this not to be the case, depending on how the endowment fund is established. This author has had the experience of helping to start a church endowment fund that grew to more than two million dollars over a seventeen-year period, while simultaneously increasing the church budget fourfold, from 120,000 dollars to 475,000 dollars! So it is possible to do both at the same time without one hurting the other.

The solution is *not* to refuse to use any endowment fund income for the ministries of a church and insist that the endowment income will only be used for building maintenance or capital needs, mission projects outside the church, or for scholarships for the young people of the church to attend college. The solution to the potential problem of having your people rely on the endowment and not giving adequately is to prepare two budgets each year: an operating budget for ministry and an endowment income budget.

The operating ministry budget underwrites the basic ministry costs of the church, including staff costs and expenses for the ministries of worship, evangelism, congregational care, Christian education, wider mission, Christian witness in society, fellowship, buildings and grounds, and stewardship—and all these are to be funded by the pledges of the people. The endowment income budget, on the other hand, is to be used for those ministries that we feel Jesus wants us to be about, but that we cannot afford them in the ministry/operating budget at this time.

This would include such things as beginning a new ministry for which there would otherwise not be adequate funds, such as a new worship service that might cost twenty thousand dollars to get off the ground, a new mission project in the area or overseas, a new part-time staff person to begin or strengthen a particular ministry, a new boiler or roof, a remodeling project for Sunday school rooms, or a new counseling service. Then plans should be made to move 20 percent of a new ministry or staff person's salary into the operating budget each year for the next five years. Make it clear to the church membership that the operating budget that is supported by the giving of the membership needs to pay for the basic ministries that it has now. The endowment income budget is to be used for those ministries that Jesus wants us to be about, but we cannot afford at this time within the operating budget.

A major mistake most churches make with their endowment fund income is to restrict its use so severely that it hampers effective ministry from occurring, when the money was given by folk who wanted it to be used for growing the ministries of the church and making them more effective! Use it for *expanding the church's ministries* beyond what you can afford out of the current operating budget. (Of course, you need to have a plan to move it into the operating budget over a reasonable time.) That's why God and the donors gave us those monies—to do as much of the work of Jesus Christ in our world today and in the future as we possibly can.

Another mistake many churches make is that they don't want to use too much of the income from the endowment fund—period! Instead, they want to grow the principal by using a large percentage of the income of the endowment by reinvesting it back into the principal.

When a church I pastored received its first gift in excess of one million dollars, it was decided to have it managed by a professional investment firm (which is a good idea). We told the investment firm that we wanted to make at least 6 percent income on our investment and to use that much for additional ministry each year. The investment person told us, "Oh, don't use so much. Let me reinvest your income, and in ten years I'll double your money!" My response was that if we were a bank or an investment firm that would probably be good advice. But we are a church of Jesus Christ, and our purpose is to do as much ministry as we can every year of our existence, and we need and want endowment fund income equal to 6 percent of the principal to use for ministry every year. Besides, the best and fastest way to grow the principal is not by putting most of the annual income back into the principal. The best and fastest way to grow the principal is to go out and ask more people if they would like to continue their ministry in their church after they die.

After we visited all of our people over eighty years of age, and spoke with them about continuing ministry gifts, our endowment fund grew from 115,000 to 2,175,000 dollars in four years, with the church receiving an additional $120,000 dollars per year for additional ministry! There is no way that reinvesting the income from the principal would have achieved those results! I would suggest to you that the reason we want to reinvest so much of the income is because we do not believe that we will receive any more gifts. We really do not believe that we live in a world with a never-ending abundance of resources. Instead, we choose to believe that we live in a world of limited resources. Of course, we also don't like the idea of going out and asking for additional gifts.

Other uses of the endowment fund income can include borrowing from your endowment fund principal (at the same interest rate it is currently making) rather than borrowing from a bank at two to four interest points higher when you need to take out a loan on a capital improvement, or providing one of your full-time clergy with a low-interest loan (2 percent) to help them with a down payment on a home in your community in the event that you do not have a parsonage. See appendix 8, "Local Church Endowment Fund Guidelines," and appendix 9, "Developing/Enhancing Endowment Funds in Local Churches."

Encouragement Letters

A fifth task of a stewardship ministry is to oversee and facilitate the timely receipt of all pledge payments via "encouragement letters" rather than "balance due statements." In declining/dying churches the financial secretary usually sends out quarterly or sometimes just annual financial statements to its members that say something like, "You have pledged _____. You have given _____. Balance Due _____." Don't say "balance due!"—that sounds like a bill coming from a store or a bank!

Instead, send quarterly "encouragement letters" with the first paragraph reading something like this, "During the past three months our church has been able to start a new Bible study class, call a part-time youth leader, and put a fresh coat of paint on Fellowship Hall because of your gifts. Thank you! Thank you! Thank you!"

The second paragraph might read, "In the next six months we want to begin training a new group of Stephen Ministers to work one-on-one with hurting persons within our congregation, as well as to begin a new evangelism ministry that will perform "random acts of kindness" for people of our area with no strings attached, and we need your help!

If the recipients of this letter are up to date or ahead on paying their pledges, the third paragraph reads, "You are providing significant leadership for our church, and we are exceedingly grateful!" If, on the other hand, the recipients of this letter are behind on their pledge payments, *do not* say, "Your pledge is in arrears! Time to catch up!" Instead, the encouragement letter says, "We know we can count on you!" (Would you mind receiving a letter like this when your pledge was "in arrears"?)

These encouragement letters are sent out by the financial secretary with a statement indicating the person's pledge and giving to date, but *without* the balance due statement. But have the encouragement letters written by the stewardship ministry people rather than the financial secretary, because financial secretaries and stewardship people often have different perspectives and feelings about overdue pledge payments.

Appreciation

A sixth task of the stewardship ministry is to develop a multitude of creative ways to express gratitude and appreciation to all who give! We don't say, "Thank you" enough in the church! We act as if our members "owe" us a pledge, and "owe" it to us to pay what they pledged on time! It's kind of like paying their "dues" for belonging to the church. The time is long gone that church members paid dues to their churches, and it's high time we stop treating our people as if they were still doing it! We Christians are to be grateful people, even when it comes to making and paying a pledge.

Thus, the day after a church member makes a pledge, a thank-you note needs to be sent (preferably written in longhand rather than typed). Too often churches wait until all the pledges are in (usually in mid-January), after which a typed, general letter is sent to all who pledged (even though some of those pledges were given in October or November). Often the letter doesn't even have a personalized greeting!

Moreover, thank your people who participate in the church's ministries. Don't wait until they have completed their two- or three-year term to thank them at a church annual meeting (which most of them do not even attend). In a church I served, we started Ye Olde Order of Footwashers to thank our servant workers. Each month in the church newsletter I chose a person or couple who had been giving their time away freely and eagerly to serve in one of our ministries, as well as in projects in the community. The newsletter declared, "The Footwasher(s) for April is/are _____ _____! Welcome to Ye Olde Order of Footwashers," after which there was a paragraph or two about what they had been doing in the church and the community so joyfully. In addition, the next Sunday they were presented with a certificate of induction into Ye Olde Order of Footwashers. Over a seventeen-year period, hundreds of persons were thanked in this way.

Coordination

A seventh task of the stewardship ministry is to coordinate the stewardship education, annual Stewardship Spiritual Growth Event, all special offerings, capital campaigns, spiritual gifts ministry, and continuing ministry gifts into an overall stewardship ministry plan for the church. This is done by having the leader of each of the stewardship teams meet with the stewardship staff person three to four times per year for the purpose of coordination, evaluation, planning, and goal setting. Other than that, we want to free up the members of the various teams to spend most of their time, effort, and energy executing/doing their ministries!

chapter eleven

Christian Education

LIVING CHURCHES

The primary mission of Christian Education is to disciple all *members—adults, youth, and children—in the way of Jesus.*

Every *member is expected and encouraged to participate in at least one discipling opportunity each year, with a large percentage of them doing so.*

A youth ministry *is developed in which youth (ages twelve to eighteen) come to know Jesus and learn to follow in his footsteps. Social, "fun" events are part of this process.*

Ongoing, "hands-on" educational experiences for children ages two to eleven are developed (Sunday school, Wednesday family night, vacation church school, etc.) using the eight methods of learning that pertain to meaningful Christian life.[1]

DYING CHURCHES

The primary mission of Christian education is to teach *children* the basic tenants of the faith.

Most adults do not attend any form of adult education. Most youth disappear following their confirmation.

A youth *fellowship* schedules a series of social, "fun" events, because that is all youth will attend.

A Sunday school for children uses a curriculum that is easy for the teacher, does not take too much time to prepare, and has the children listening to the teacher talk and participating in crafts not necessarily related to meaningful Christian life.

IN THE GREAT COMMISSION JESUS SAID, "Go . . . and *make disciples* of all nations . . . teaching them to obey everything that I have commanded you" (Matt. 28:19, 20). Yet in mainline Protestant churches "making disciples" has not been at the forefront of the focus of our educational endeavors. We don't even like the word! It sounds too "evangelical!"

Rather than helping our children come to know Jesus and to want to be like him, over the years we have been more concerned that they memorize some Bible passages, learn the Lord's Prayer and Apostles Creed, memorize the books of the Bible, build some buildings like they had in Bible times, come to know some of the Old and New Testament stories and personages, or work on crafts that may have little or nothing to do with coming to know Jesus and being like him.

Similarly, discipling our youth in the way of Jesus also has not been the focus of our work with them. Instead, too often it has been centered around keeping them off the streets and in the church by offering a series of "fun" events such as bowling one week, ice skating the next, then having a pizza party, going to Six Flags Amusement Park, and so on. Of course, we need to do these things with youth, but as part of a total program centered in helping them to know Jesus, to love him, and to follow his way!

In like manner, the focus of our adult education has not been primarily that of discipling them in the way of Jesus. Instead, probably because it has been difficult to get adults to participate in adult education, we have tended to offer a potpourri of electives that might connect with someone's interest at one time or another. So we might have classses on parenting, the marital relationship, handling conflict, learning to meditate, other religions, a Bible study here or there, or we might offer a video series on one topic or another. Yet, in spite of these "supermarket" attempts to get adults into educational experiences, we still have very few takers! Too often there is no well-defined, overall plan to disciple our adults, to help them know Jesus, to enflesh his living Spirit, and to follow his way more closely. In fact, my own observation over forty-plus years of ministry is that we in the mainline churches don't talk about Jesus very much at all of late. We use a lot of "God talk," but we have been shying away from using the name of Jesus. Do we think it sounds too "evangelical" to speak of him? Was it not Paul who said, "God gave Jesus the name that is above every name, so that at the name of Jesus every knee should bow and every tongue confess that Jesus Christ is Lord?" (Phil. 2:9–11).

On the other hand, in growing/living churches the "discipling" of its members is a major mission of the church. The mission statement of Frazier United Methodist Church in Montgomery, Alabama, has but three words, "Win! Disciple! Serve!" which means "Win people for Christ! Disciple them in the Way of Christ! Serve the world in the name and Spirit of Christ!" Thus, in this church the discipling of its members is one of the three basic tasks that need to be undertaken.

Moreover, discipling involves training its members in ministry within the church, after helping them to know Jesus and to follow his way. I was most impressed the first time I attended the Garden Grove Community Church, now known primarily as the Crystal Cathedral, in Garden Grove, California. What impressed me more than the buildings and grounds was the fact that they had three hundred well-trained laity serving as ministers of pastoral care calling on the hospitalized and homebound, three hundred well-trained laity functioning as ministers of evangelism following up on visitors who attended the church, three hundred or so well-trained laity who were ministers of hospitality, and approximately one hundred well-trained laity serving in their telephone hotline ministry being a listening friend to all who called in with their problems and troubles. When I asked some of them what was going to happen at their church when Bob Schuller retired or died, each of them answered "We have a lot more going here than Bob Schuller! He has seen that we have been discipled in the way of Jesus and trained to do his ministries! When he is gone, we will continue to do ministry as we are now!" Bob Schuller has carried out the biblical mandate for pastors by "equipping the saints for ministry."

Similarly, growing/living churches develop a youth "ministry" as opposed to a youth "fellowship." Again, they see their primary mission as discipling their youth by helping them to know Jesus, to enflesh his living Spirit, and to follow his way more closely. Thus, they engage their youth in contemporary worship using their language, music, and technology; in Bible study; in a multitude of service opportunities, retreats, work camps, and work trips to see how "the least of these" live, as well as coming to know and work alongside them; and having some "fun" events. Moreover, Sunday morning classes, a Confirmation program that prepares the youth for making their own intentional decisions to become followers of Jesus, and youth choirs, praise teams, and bands are all considered part of the youth ministry.

Folk in dying churches, on the other hand, think that if they did anything but "fun" events, no one would come. But the fact is that youth want something more significant to happen than just to have fun, and the record shows that churches that do youth *ministry* have many youth coming, whereas churches that do youth *fellowship* based primarily on fun events, have few coming!

Regarding the Christian education of children, growing/living churches tend to have a number of regular educational experiences for those two to eleven years of age, such as a Sunday and/or Saturday school or "Kids Klub," a Wednesday family night, vacation church school, and similar programs.

Each of the different educational experiences selects a curriculum that engages the children in coming to know Jesus and what it means to follow him. Moreover, the various curricula are coordinated so as to not duplicate topics, activities, and the like. "Hands on" methods are used as opposed to just listening to the teacher speak, and the eight different styles of learning are utilized since all people, including children, learn in different ways. This is referred to as the Workshop Rotation Style.[2]

In addition, living churches get the parents involved at home in the discipling/learning process so that what happens at the church is continued and expanded in the home setting. After all, the children spend much more time at home than at church, and the parents need to be involved in their children's Christian discipling.

chapter twelve

Pastoral (Congregational) Care

LIVING CHURCHES	DYING CHURCHES
Pastors train spiritually gifted laity to do pastoral (congregational) care.	It is the pastor's job to do pastoral care!

IN DECLINING/DYING CHURCHES, the prevailing thinking among the membership is that they pay the pastor(s) to visit the sick, hospitalized, and homebound and counsel everyone in the congregation who has a problem of any kind. After all, most mainline church constitutions read as follows: "It shall be the duty of the pastor(s) to conduct worship services, direct the work of Christian education, administer the Holy Sacraments, visit the sick, comfort the distressed, seek new members, and perform such duties as belong to the pastor(s) office."

But in the growing/living church the pastors take their biblical role seriously of "equipping the saints for ministry" (Eph. 4:12). This is the model Jesus gave to us. First he discipled his followers to follow his way and, second, he trained them to do the same ministries he did by first sending out the twelve, and then later sending seventy others, to share the good news of the coming of the realm of God to earth in their time (which occurred whenever people obeyed and allowed God to be their ruler), to free people of that which was enslaving them and keeping them from living in the realm of God in the present, and to heal their deafness of being unable to hear the messages of Jesus and of their blindness to seeing the new possibilities for their lives—making them whole again in body and spirit.

Similarly, when St. Paul started churches throughout Asia Minor (present-day Turkey) and Greece, he first sought to disciple the people in the Spirit and way of Jesus, and then he trained them to do the same ministries he did so that he could go on and start new communities of Jesus' followers. He did, however, revisit these churches to continue to teach and train them, and he used his letters to them to continue education and training.

There is the model for pastors today! First, disciple your people in the Spirit and way of Jesus, and then train them—equip them—to do the work of Jesus' ministries. Do that for the same reasons Jesus and Paul did—many more people can be reached by many workers than by one. Much more can be accomplished on behalf of the realm of God on earth much faster by many people than by one! Congregational care means congregation members taking on the roles of caring for other members of the congregation.

In growing/living churches pastors disciple and train the persons who have the biblical spiritual gifts of caring and compassion to visit the sick, the hospitalized, and homebound. These people learn skills such as how to listen to others and respond, which scriptures can be helpful, and how to pray with others. For those who wish to be trained even more, the church can institute a Stephen's Ministry to prepare individuals to be listening friends and supporters of hurting individuals over a longer period of time. In a church I served, we had thirty-five pastoral care callers and more than forty Stephen's Ministers. Seventy-five people did so much more than my two associate pastors and I could have possibly done! Of course, a pastor also visits the sick, hospitalized, and homebound, as well as counsels. But the ministry is so much stronger when many others are doing it in addition to the pastor(s).

There are many other pastoral (congregational) care ministries that need to be developed and for which trained laity are needed, for example, sending and delivering cards, gifts, and flowers to the hospitalized and homebound; a transportation corps to help get those who can no longer drive to the doctor, grocery store, bank, and other places; and development of support groups for widows/widowers, singles, and recently divorced persons. Living churches have dozens (even hundreds) of people working in the ministry of pastoral (congregational) care in their churches.

chapter thirteen

Wider Mission

LIVING CHURCHES	DYING CHURCHES
The congregation is significantly monetarily invested and personally involved in being God's servants among God's children who are suffering throughout the world.	The congregation has a low monetary investment and personal involvement beyond their own church.
The congregation has a passion for enabling all of God's children to experience God's plan for this world of "shalom" (justice, peace, unity, prosperity).	The congregation believes that Christians and churches should stay out of politics and social justice issues since they are divisive.

I USE THE TERM "WIDER MISSION" as opposed to the term "mission" for ministries aimed at reaching folk in the wider world beyond the local church because *all* of the ministries of the church are part of the mission of the church of Jesus Christ. The mission of the church, the basic purpose, the business of the church is to fulfill *all* of the ministries of Jesus in the world today—to share the good news of life in Christ Jesus and bring all people under the authority of God; to provide worship opportunities that communicate with all generations; to disciple our children, youth, and adults; to care for the well-being of our members; to develop faithful stewards of God's abundance; to have care and compassion for those who are hurting throughout the world; to help bring

God's created "shalom" back into our world; and to provide the necessary buildings and grounds to enable all the other ministries of the church to occur. If we use the word "mission" only for those ministries that reach beyond the walls of the church it implies, even states, that all the other ministries are not part and parcel of the mission of the church of Jesus Christ.

There are some mainline Protestants who maintain that the ministries of evangelism and wider mission (especially that of Christian witness in society) cannot coexist within a church, that pursuing new members keeps a church from engaging in ministries that might be divisive. Conversely, they say, very active participation in wider mission ministries (especially advocating for peace and justice) makes churches lose members rather than gain them.

But my experience with hundreds of mainline churches over the past ten years reveals just the opposite. Those churches that are heavily invested monetarily and personally in service ministries to the "least of these," as well as in advocacy ministries on behalf of restoring God's created world of "shalom," are the growing/living churches. On the other hand, those churches that have a small monetary and personal involvement in service ministries, and no involvement in ministries of advocacy on behalf of "shalom," are declining/dying churches.

Of course, those mainline churches are also declining/dying that see the engagement in social justice and peace issues as the primary mission of the church, often to the disparagement and almost total neglect of evangelism and other ministries; those churches that "baptize" every pronouncement emanating from their state and national judicatories (believing that a given pronouncement is exactly what God wants regarding each issue, and ignoring the necessity of compromise in politics as Reinhold Niebuhr taught us so long ago)[1]; and those churches that then force their members to vote up or down on those pronouncements (with 51 percent of the vote dictating what that church believes and where it stands, thereby coercing the other 49 percent to go along with them).

But those mainline churches are thriving that see evangelism as the primary mission of the church but at the same time have a wholistic view that all of the ministries of the church are crucially important, with each performing an absolutely necessary role in the body of Christ here on earth (1 Cor. 12). Those mainline churches are thriving that carefully review each pronouncement emanating from the higher judicatories, but don't "baptize" them, and instead have discussion sessions where all are listened to and heard from, all are respected, and all attempt to come to some consensus based on their understandings of the will and way of God as revealed through Jesus.

Declining/dying churches usually want nothing to do with justice and peace ministries whatsoever because they believe that they can be divisive. This is to deny that Jesus wants us to do as he did when he said, "The Spirit of the Lord is upon me, because he has anointed me to bring good news to the poor. He has sent me to proclaim release to the captives and recovery of sight to the blind, to let the oppressed go free" (Luke 4:18). This is another of the ministries of Jesus in which we must be involved for it is as crucially important as worship, Christian education, pastoral care, or any other ministry. In the body of Christ if one or more of the ministries is not functioning as Jesus wants, then the entire work of the body is harmed. Jesus never refused to do what God wanted because it could be divisive! We will never find that as an acceptable excuse in our Bibles for not participating in a ministry of Jesus.

Declining/dying churches also give very little money "away" to help others outside their church fellowship. We often hear from them that "charity begins at home." Thus, at best, these churches give no more than they absolutely have to, often amounting to less than 1 percent of their church budgets. In fact, many churches give no money from their church budgets whatsoever, instead giving away only that which is donated separately by their members to certain causes. These churches usually give the least of all. Churches decline and die if they do not believe Jesus when he said, "Give, and it will be given to you. A good measure, pressed down, shaken together, running over, will be put in your lap; for the measure you give will be the measure you get back" (Luke 6:38). Declining/dying churches don't have enough to give, because they haven't given enough away!

Conversely, growing/living churches freely and eagerly give away great amounts of money to help the poor, hungry, homeless, those discriminated against, the aged, the mentally ill, and others in need, not because they have a lot of money, but because they feel it is the will of God, it is like Jesus, to care passionately for those who have the least. I know one church that gave away more than 150,000 dollars in 2001 for these purposes. This was a church with a 600,000-dollar budget, with a good chunk of the 150,000 dollars coming from the budget and the rest coming from designated giving by the members, as well as some from the endowment fund.

Moreover, in growing/living churches many members (and non-members) are personally and passionately involved in wider mission ministries, working in shelters for the homeless, volunteering in food pantries and clothes closets, helping to build houses through Habitat for Humanity, mentoring homeless people as they move into apartments (which are paid for by these churches), going on learning/work trips to foreign lands, and to various places with high poverty levels in our nation. I know one church that not only houses the homeless every Monday night from October through April, but also spent 15,000 dollars purchasing and installing a shower and washer and dryer off their fellowship hall so that their homeless guests could bathe and wash their clothes. Growing/living churches want to do "hands on" ministry, in addition to giving away their money to help others.

chapter fourteen

Church Buildings and Property

LIVING CHURCHES

The church buildings and property are seen as tools and servants of all the other ministries of the church.

DYING CHURCHES

The church buildings and property are seen as ends in themselves, often becoming "sacred cows."

O VER THE PAST TEN YEARS AS A STATE church conference judicatory staff person and as a consultant with churches throughout much of the United States, I have seen many beautiful church buildings, but many of them have little significant ministry going on within them. Often these churches have one poorly attended worship service on Sunday mornings with a handful of children attending Sunday school (although sometimes that has already folded).

In addition, they may have a women's fellowship struggling to survive since most of the attendees are getting too old to carry on some of the significant things they used to do. They usually still have an altar guild (often down to one or two people), who see that there are flowers on the altar on Sundays, prepare the communion elements, and wash the dishes, and, of course, they have a group of men whose mission is to keep the building and grounds in top shape. The preservation of that building and those grounds has obviously become that church's primary mission. The building and grounds budget in a church like this is often more than half the budget, even more than the combined salaries and benefits of the staff! The buildings and grounds have become a "sacred cow."

Moreover, in dying churches that still have a youth group or sponsor a Boy Scout troop, if the youth mar the paint on the walls in the midst of their activities or the Boy Scouts poke holes in the tiled ceilings when they place their flags in the flag stands, then they are banned forever from the fellowship hall! The building is more important than the ministries occurring within it—it takes precedence over everything else. The buildings and grounds have become a "sacred cow."

Many mainline Protestant church buildings are now or are getting close to one hundred years old. They were built at a time when people walked or came by horse and buggy to church. Thus, many are sitting on a small piece of land with little or no off-street parking. The buildings often have steep, narrow stairways upon entering the church, as well as within. The sanctuary is too small to enable the congregation to grow, or in some situations it is so large that the tiny congregation gets lost within its cavernous space. The chancel area is often extremely small and crowded, even with just an altar, pulpit, and lectern on it. Thus, there may be no room for a screen with which to have visuals, nor is there room for drama, dance, or much else. It was designed solely for having a person read or speak to the congregation and serve communion. There is little or no flexibility within the worship space. In addition, the Sunday school rooms tend to be too small for adequate Christian education to occur; and the fellowship hall is small, dingy, and smells musty from decades of mold.

Yet many congregations refuse to seriously consider the option of tearing the old building down and building a new, beautiful, functional building; or worse yet, they refuse to even think about the possibility of relocating the church to a much larger piece of property that would provide adequate parking, be in a more advantageous location for evangelism (at an intersection with a good deal of daily traffic), and be a good functional tool for all the new and creative ministries that the congregation needs to be about in this new time. Witness how fast-food franchises, banks, office buildings, and many stores tear down or remodel their buildings every ten years or so, because they are no longer functional in our rapidly changing environment. Yet, we insist on hanging on to church buildings that became dysfunctional fifty years ago and more!

Why do congregations resist the idea of relocation so strongly? Because "I grew up and was baptized and confirmed in this church building!" "My spouse and I were married in this sanctuary and our children were baptized here!" "My spouse's funeral was held here!" "This is home!" (There are usually a hundred other reasons given as well, often many of them disguising the real one: "I don't want to spend the added money!")

Thus, the building, grounds, and location have become the most important mission of the church, although these cannot be found within the Bible as the church's mission! The building, grounds, and location have become a "sacred cow" that takes precedence over everything else, even over Jesus' Great Commission of to go to all people everywhere making them disciples, even over Jesus' call to his disciples to catch people by the netful for life in the realm of God here on earth. This church is a dying church! It has died to the mission of the church of Jesus Christ and instituted its own mission—"We must save our building, grounds, and location above everything else!"

The growing/living church, on the other hand, does not view the church buildings, grounds, and location as ends in themselves, or as more important than everything else. Instead, they see the buildings, grounds, and location as tools for all the ministries of Christ's church to function at their highest levels; they are servants of all the other ministries of the church to help them fulfill the overall, basic mission of the church of Jesus Christ (evangelism), as well as the specific missions of each of the other ministries.

If the existing building can be effectively remodeled for worship that can reach the unchurched/dechurched younger generations of our time; if adequate space can be developed for discipling our adults, youth, and children; if it is possible to make the entirety of all the buildings accessible to all folk; if adequate space can be developed for genuine youth ministry, outreach ministries to the homeless and hungry, and support groups; and if the parking lot can be significantly expanded, then the growing/living church will do whatever it takes to update and upgrade the facilities accordingly.

However, if the existing buildings, grounds, and location cannot be effectively remodeled to meet the needs just listed, then the growing/living church will seek to relocate to another site where the mission of the church of Jesus Christ, and the mission of this church, can be accomplished! Thus, the buildings, grounds, and location are tools and servants of the mission of the church, rather than ends in themselves—rather than "sacred cows!"

resource

Does Your Church Need Help?

IF YOUR CHURCH WOULD LIKE SOME HELP IN

- developing a new vision for your church's future;

- creating an effective mission statement and some concrete strategies to start moving toward accomplishing your mission and achieving your vision;

- reorganizing your church structures for more effective ministries in the twenty-first century

- developing ministries of evangelism and worship that will reach the unchurched, dechurched, and younger generations of our time;

- establishing a ministry of stewardship based on biblical principles that will provide the necessary people and financial resources your church needs to be a vital, living church once again,

contact Rev. Dr. Robert Schieler at 3114 Whispering Oaks Lane, Woodridge, IL 60517, 630-910-3837; or e-mail <rcschieler@aol.com>.

Dr. Schieler will come to your church and work with your pastor(s) and lay leaders at low, affordable costs. You may also arrange for several of your area churches to gather to deal with one or more of the crucial issues listed above to help turn their churches around from dying to living churches once more!

Appendix 1

Blended Contemporary/
Traditional Worship Service

THIS SERVICE IS DESIGNED to reach the "establishment" and "baby boomer" generations (Persons aged fifty-five and older, with some church background). It is believer-oriented, but visitor friendly. Spirited-traditional services (another name for these blended services) maintain the beauty, dignity, and order of liturgical worship, while adding appropriate contemporary elements. "Spirited" emphasizes energy, joy, and celebration and reaches out to the younger generations. "Traditional" reminds us of our ties with past generations of believers.

Theme: "When the Holy Spirit Comes Upon You . . ."

Call to Worship:
"This is Holy Ground"
(Christopher Beatty © copyright 1982, arr. 1986
Birdway Music/Sparrow)

Welcome: liturgist

ADORATION AND PRAISE

Hymn of Praise (sing in unison):
"Spirit, Spirit of Gentleness"
(James K. Maulay, 1978, *The New Century Hymnal*,
The United Church of Christ) or another similar song

Testimonies of Praise: (responsively)

Liturgust:	We praise you, O God, for your ever-present Spirit
Congregation:	**which is all around us and resides deep within us**
Liturgust:	which keeps calling us to move ever forward
Congregation:	**to become all that you want us to be as persons, as your church, and as a world community!**
Liturgust:	We praise you, O God, for your ever-present Spirit
Congregation:	**which gives us glimpses, dreams, and visions of the new things you are doing in this new time and inviting us to join you in them!**

Songs of Praise: (Praise Team and Congregation)

"This is the Day"
(Les Garrett, 1967, *The New Century Hymnal*,
The United Church of Christ)

"Jesus, Name above All Names"
(Naida Hearn, © copyright 1974, arr. 1986 Scripture in Song)

"We Will Glorify"
(Twila Paris © copyright 1982, arr. 1986 Singspiration Music)

"Spirit Song"
(John Wimber, © copyright 1979 Mercy Publishing)

CONFESSION

Confession of Sin: (in unison)

We confess, O God, that we often resist your calls
to move forward, to change, to be and do things differently,
    to take risks and venture into an unknown future.
We prefer the comfort and security of the familiar, the habitual.

We shy away from the risks, work, and costs involved
  in following the great dreams and visions you give us.
We need your living Spirit
  to give us the faith and courage
  to follow where you are leading us.

Confession Response: (sing in unison):

"Change My Heart, O God"
(Eddie Espinosa, © copyright 1982, 1987 Mercy Publishing)

FORGIVENESS

Good News of Forgiveness: (liturgist)

If you truly mean what you have just prayed,
  then our good God forgives you!
The past is finished and gone!
Everything has become fresh and new!
Believe this good news
  and forgive yourself!

Response of Thanksgiving:

"Blessed Assurance"
(Fanny Crosby, 1873)

First verse: saxophone solo, followed by the praise team
                    and congregation:

HEARING THE WORD OF GOD

Scripture Readings (read in unison):

When the Holy Spirit comes upon you,
  you will be filled with power,
  and you will be witnesses for me
  in Jerusalem, in all of Judea and Samaria,
  and to the ends of the earth (Acts 1:8)

Many of them believed Peter's message and were baptized,
  and about three thousand people were added to the group that day.

They spent their time in learning from the apostles, taking part in the
  fellowship,
    and sharing in the fellowship meals and the prayers.
Many miracles and wonders were being done through the apostles,
    and everyone was filled with awe.
All the believers continued together in close fellowship
    and shared their belongings with one another.
They would sell their possessions
    and distribute the money among all, according to what each needed.
Day after day they met as a group in the Temple,
    and they had their meals together in their homes,
    eating with glad and humble hearts,
    praising God, and enjoying the good will of all people.
And every day the Lord added to their group
    those who were being saved. (Acts 2:41–47)

Message: "When the Holy Spirit Comes Upon You . . ."

COMMITMENT

Song of Praise:
                "Spirit of the Living God"
    (Daniel Iverson, © copyright 1935, renewal 1965, Birdsong
                    Music/Sparrow)

A TIME OF PRAYER

PASTORAL PRAYER

THE LORD'S PRAYER (IN UNISON)

    Our Father, who art in heaven, hallowed be thy name.
    Thy Kingdom come, thy will be done on earth, as it is in
    heaven.
    Give us this day our daily bread,
    and forgive us our debts, as we forgive our debtors.
    And lead us not into temptation, but deliver us from evil,
    for thine is the kingdom, and the power, and the glory forever.
    Amen.

Prayer Response:

"Sole Desire"
(Walt Harrrah, © copyright 1992, Maranatha Music)
sung by praise team

HYMN OF COMMITMENT:

"Sweet, Sweet Spirit"
(Doris Akers, 1962, *The New Century Hymnal*,
The United Church of Christ)

Benediction: All hold hands and sing

Alleluia, alleluia, alleluia, alleluia

(hum three alleluias while benediction is given;
sing—last "alleluia")

Postlude: "Every Time I Feel the Spirit"
(African American spiritual)

Every attempt has been made to use inclusive language. When Jesus is referred to as Lord, the male pronoun has been retained.

Principles of a Traditional/Contemporary Blended

WORSHIP SERVICE

1. It *is possible* to blend traditional and contemporary elements in the same worship service. Some churches have been doing this for twenty-plus years and are growing and reaching a good number of the baby boomer generation, as well as meeting the needs of those born before 1946.

2. This service is designed for your current church members, the dechurched, and some unchurched boomers.

3 Traditional elements in this type of service:

- communion table, cross, Bible
- use of robes/gowns
- printed bulletin

- some traditional hymns/anthems
- traditional liturgical elements: Prelude, Call to Worship, Confession, Assurance of Pardon, Scripture, Sermon, Pastoral Prayer, Benediction, Postlude
- organ, but use it along with a variety of other instruments

4. Contemporary elements of this type of service:
   - praise team to lead congregational singing
   - series of praise songs (with repetition)
   - some traditional hymns with contemporary arrangements/improvisation
   - only two verses of a traditional hymn
   - variety of instruments
   - several musical groups
   - liturgy is written in new, fresh style, not "canned" (taken from Book of Worship or written in a similar style)
   - words printed for Lord's Prayer (also Gloria Patri or Doxology if you use them) for unchurched
   - only one (or two) scripture readings (not all four lectionary readings)
   - words for songs projected on screen on occasion
   - use at least one-third contemporary music
   - dramatic flow/timing—no interludes more than five seconds where little or nothing happens other than worship leaders walking from one place to the other
   - banners (following a trend begun in the 1960s)

Appendix 2

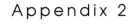

A Boomer Worship Service

THIS SERVICE SEEKS TO PRESENT the good news of life in the Spirit of Jesus in the language, music, style, and technology of the baby boomer generation (born 1946–1964). Most of the older boomers were baptized and confirmed in the church, but many of those since left it and became dechurched. This service is built around a theme that affects their daily lives, then relates the good news of our faith to that theme. Normally, there would not be a long, detailed bulletin as described below, just the basic parts of the service. The words to the songs and scripture would be projected on a screen.

Theme: "No Longer Possessed By My Possessions"

GATHERING MUSIC BY PRAISE BAND AND PRAISE TEAM

"Give Thanks"
(Henry Smith, © copyright 1978, Integrity's Hosanna! Music)

"I Love You, Lord"
Laurie Klein © copyright 1978, House of Mercy Music/
Maranatha! Music)

WELCOME AND THEME OF SERVICE

Song/Dance:
"As the Deer"
(Martin Nystrom, © copyright 1984, Maranatha! Music)

solo, with praise team, accompanied by dancer

Video: excerpts from "Affluenza"

Scripture (read in unison):
    A man in the crowd said to Jesus,
    "Teacher, tell my brother to divide with me
    the property our father left us."
    Jesus answered him, "Who gave me the right
        to judge or to divide the property between you two?"
    And he went on to say to them all,
    "Watch out and guard yourselves from every kind of greed:
        because a person's true life is not made up of the things
            one owns,
        no matter how rich one may be."
                            (Luke 12:13–15, Good News Bible)

Drama and Message: "Freed From Being Possessed by My
                    Possessions!"

Song:
                    "My Life is in You, Lord"
    (Daniel Gardner, © copyright 1986, Integrity's Hosanna! Music)

Closing Song:
"I Thank You, Jesus" (Kenneth Morris, 1948, *The New Century
        Hymnal*, The United Church of Christ)

Exit Music: praise band

*Every attempt has been made to use inclusive language. When Jesus is
referred to as Lord, the male pronoun has been retained.*

Principles of a Worship Service to Reach Baby Boomers

1. It is recommended that this type of boomer service be scheduled separately and in addition to the traditional service.

2. This service is aimed at reaching primarily unchurched/dechurched people (although a good number of your current members will like this service as well).

3. Contemporary elements in this service include:

   - created by a worship team of pastor and directors of music, drama, and audio-visuals
   - series of praise songs sung one after the other with repetition of a given song
   - no printed group prayers, responsive readings
   - praise team to lead congregational singing
   - variety of instruments (electronic keyboard, guitars, drums)
   - several musical/dramatic/dance groups in each service
   - words on screen, not in bulletin
   - all contemporary music (composed within the last thirty years)
   - good dramatic flow/timing (no interludes of more than five seconds when nothing happens)
   - one or two short scripture readings (can be projected on screen)
   - no altar, communion table, symbols (which unchurched do not know or appreciate)
   - no robes/gowns
   - excellence/quality in all that happens in the service

A Generation X Worship Service

"What Are You Going to Do With What You Have Been Given?"

The Line-Up
Song by the Sheesh Band

WELCOME
Unfolding of the Day's Theme

Visuals of gen X at work and play

Song by the Sheesh Band

Announcements
Groups and ministries available
(see on other side)

Song by the Sheesh Band

"The Secret of My Success"
—A mini-drama

Discussion of the drama and theme

Song by the Sheesh Band

Principles of a Worship Service to Reach Generation X

1. This type of service needs to be separate, in addition to, at a different time, than your other services. Most of the folks born before 1946 will not appreciate this music, but then most of generation X doesn't appreciate traditional church music either.

2. This service is aimed at reaching unchurched generation X persons, attempting to reach them with their music, their thought patterns, dealing with their issues at their growing edges.

3. Contemporary elements in this service include:

   - hard rock music (loud)

   - a "gen X" band

   - very informal, very casual

   - no gowns, symbols of the faith, etc.

   - use of a theme that deals with issues affecting them,such as "What are you going to do with what you have been given?"

   - a number of opportunities available outside of worship to connect with these people—inquiry groups, connecting groups, compassion groups, "hang out time"

   - multimedia/multivisual/multisensory presentation (ala MTV) is meaningful to generation X. This is the first "visual" as opposed to "print" generation"

   - drama from everyday life appeals to generation X— looking for the real, authentic "experiences" they want

Appendix 4

~~~~~~~~

Scripture Passages on Stewardship

THESE SCRIPTURE PASSAGES and paraphrases can be used for Bible studies, sermons, adult classes, and in stewardship campaigns.

Leviticus 19:9, 10	When you harvest your fields, leave some for the poor.
Deuteronomy 6:10–13	Don't forget that God gave you everything you have!
1 Chronicles 29:1–20	David's example of a good steward in the building of the temple is an excellent illustration of how to conduct a capital campaign.
Psalm 24:1, 2	The world and all that is in it belongs to God.
Psalm 34:8–10	Those who obey God have all they need.
Psalm 65	What a rich harvest God's goodness provides!
Psalm 145:13–21	God provides all living things with food and satisfies the needs of all.
Proverbs 11:25	Be generous and you will be prosperous!

Proverbs 14:21	If you want to be happy, be kind to the poor.
Proverbs 15:16	Better to be poor and fear God than to be rich and in trouble.
Proverbs 19:17	When you give to the poor, it is like lending to God.
Proverbs 21:6	The riches you get by dishonesty soon disappear.
Proverbs 22:9	Be generous and share your food with the poor.
Proverbs 30:8	Let me neither be rich or poor. Give me only the food I need.
Malachi 3:10	Bring your tithes to the temple . . . and God will pour out abundance!
Matthew 6:25–34	Don't worry about food, clothing, and the like. God will provide.
Matthew 25:14-30	Parable of the talents: How does God want us to use what God gives us?
Luke 6:38	The measure you give will be the measure you receive.
Luke 12:13–15	A person's true life is not made up of things one owns.
Luke 12:16–21	Parable of the rich fool. What does this say regarding the "American dream" of making as much as fast as we can, so we can retire early and have fun?
Luke 12:32–34	Your heart is where your treasures are.
Luke 12:42–48	Parable of the faithful and unfaithful servant (steward). How does God want us to manage (steward) what God puts in our care?

Luke 12:48	Much is required from the person to whom much is given!
Luke 13:6–8	Parable of the unfruitful fig tree: What happens when we don't bear fruit with what we've been given?
Luke 16:1–12	Parable of the shrewd steward: Learn how to handle worldly wealth so you will attain eternal wealth.
Luke 16:13	We cannot serve both God and money!
Luke 16:19–31	The rich man and Lazarus
Luke 18:18–27	How hard it is for rich people to enter God's realm.
Luke 19:1–9	Jesus and Zacchaeus
Luke 21:1–3	The poor widow who gave all she had.
Mark 6:30–51	Feeding of the five thousand and the disciples in the sinking boat.
Mark 8:1–10, 14–21	Feeding of the four thousand and the disciples in the boat.
1 Corinthians 16:1, 2	Each Sunday, put aside some money in proportion to what you have been given.
1 Corinthians 10:31–33	Whatever you do—eat, drink, etc.—do all to the glory of God.
1 Corinthians 12:4–13	God gives all of us spiritual gifts to use in God's service.
2 Corinthians 8:1–5	Even though they were very poor, the Macedonians begged and pleaded for the opportunity to give!
2 Corinthians 9:6	We will reap as we sow—sparingly or bountifully.

2 Corinthians 9:7, 8	God will give you all you need and enough for every good cause.
2 Corinthians 9:10–15	Your generosity will lead to an outpouring of gratitude to God.
1 Timothy 6:5b–10	The love of money is the root of all evil.
1 Timothy 6:7–19	Those who are rich must be generous and do good works in order to have true life.

Appendix 5

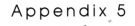

Stewardship "One-Liners"

USE THESE CATCHY ONE-LINERS in worship bulletins, newsletters, and other printed material to promote stewardship.

- "You cannot outgive God!"
- "Give, and it will be given to you." (Luke 6:38)
- "The measure you give will be the measure you get back." (Luke 6:38)
- "The one who sows sparingly will reap sparingly!" (2 Cor. 9:6)
- "The one who sows bountifully will also reap bountifully!" (2 Cor. 9:6)
- "Each of you must give . . . not reluctantly or under compulsion, for God loves a cheerful giver." (2 Cor. 9:7)
- "God is able to provide you with every blessing in abundance, so that by always having enough of everything, you may share abundantly in every good work." (2 Cor. 9:8)
- "You glorify God by your obedience . . . and by your generosity of your sharing with them and with all others." (2 Cor. 9:13)
- "From everyone to whom much has been given, much will be required; and from the one to whom much has been entrusted, even more will be demanded." (Luke 12:48)
- "Do not worry about your life, what you will eat, or about your body, what you will wear. . . . Your Father knows that you need them. Instead, strive for his kingdom, and these things will be given to you as well." (Luke 12:22b, 30b–31)

- "For where your treasure is, there your heart will be also." (Luke 12:34)

- "Take care! Be on your guard against all kinds of greed; for one's life does not consist in the abundance of possessions." (Luke 12:15)

- "Bring the full tithe into the storehouse . . . see if I will not open the windows of heaven for you and pour down for you an overflowing blessing." (Mal. 3:10)

- "No one claimed private ownership of any possessions, but everything they owned was held in common. . . . and great grace was upon them all." (Acts 4:32, 33)

- Let us give according to our incomes, lest God make our incomes match our gifts!—Peter Marshall

- There is nothing to fear or lose by giving, for God will always give you more than you give!—Robert Schieler

Effective Stewardship Spiritual Growth Events (Campaigns)

Goals

1. Teach biblical stewardship in each event (campaign). Every important decision we make in life is a stewardship decision. "What are we going to do with what God has given us?" God is the owner of all there is and we are God's stewards to manage on behalf of God all that we are and have been given.

   - change perspectives/thinking (from self-centered, worldly perspectives to Godly perspectives)

   - transform lives

2. Help each church member develop a "giving spirit," or "giving attitude" to be more like God (made in God's giving image). Do *not* ask people to give to pay bills or support a budget, but to give because as humans we have a basic need to give to become more like God.

3. Help people discern their spiritual gifts and follow God's command that all—not just a few elected leaders—are to use their gifts in ministry.

4. Help persons use the tithe as a "spiritual discipline" to become the givers God intends them to be.

5. Provide the necessary people and financial resources to enable the church of Jesus Christ to be what God desires and what it *can be*!

6. Open up the "conspiracy of silence" regarding money and possessions. Giving of selves, money, and possessions needs to be openly dealt with, preached about, and discussed in the life of the church. After all, Jesus spoke of these things in 30 percent of his sayings and twenty-one of his thirty-nine teaching parables.

Levels of Effectiveness

Here are different approaches to annual stewardship spiritual growth events (campaign), from most effective to least effective.

1. "From Membership to Discipleship"—two-year, all-church theme (this is the most effective)

   • visit all member households with flip charts, handouts

   • help members 1) grow spiritually, 2) discern and use their spiritual gifts in ministry, and 3) and grow in their financial giving

   • use different approaches with different groups of people

      a. learning to walk in stewardship (0–$399) (step up one $100 step)

      b. toddlers in stewardship ($400–999) (encourage to move up .5–1 percent of household income)

      c. runners/leapers/dancers in stewardship ($1,000 or more; encourage to achieve the full tithe)

2. Visit one-third of member households (visit total over three years)

   • emphasize two areas: discern and use their spiritual gifts in ministry, and grow in financial giving

   • use flip charts or video tapes and handouts in visits

   • use different approaches with different groups of people (learning to walk, toddlers, runners/leapers/ dancers)

- hold church dinners, cottage meetings, or video presentations for those not visited
- mount a letter campaign for those missed with follow-up of letters

3. Visit church leaders, people on the edge of growth, those with most potential for giving substantially
   - emphasize two areas: discern and use their spiritual gifts in ministry, and grow in financial giving
   - use flip charts or video tapes and handouts
   - use different approaches with the different groups: leaders (leaders must lead), those on the edge of growth, and those with the most potential for substantial gifts
   - hold church dinners, cottage meetings, or video presentations for those not visited
   - mount a letter campaign for those missed with follow-up of letters

4. Consecrating stewards (15–30 percent increase in first year)
   - do not ask people to pay bills or support budget, ask people to give because they have a need to give to be like God, and therefore, fully human
   - select three witnessing stewards
   - select one guest steward
   - hold a leaders' gathering ("leaders must lead" and get out "an Easter attendance")
   - use Consecration Sunday—make out pledges within worship services (pass out pledge cards within service)
   - follow up the next Sunday for those not there
   - follow up those missed by letter and pledge
   - follow up letter with calls

5. Pony Express/Run for the Roses/Family Album
   - pass saddlebags, packets, picture album from house to house

- appoint "trail bosses" for every ten houses (keep moving every twenty-four hours)
- don't let saddlebags, packets, or album get stuck for several days
- advantages: get more people to pledge (good for two to three years only)
- disadvantages: little opportunity for learning about stewardship

6. Sunday worship presentation/church dinners/cottage meetings (You will usually get most people in Sunday worship, next most for a dinner, least to cottage meetings.)
   - have Bible studies at each
   - give a video presentation on ministries of church and/or stewardship education (good video—"Affluenza")
   - have people fill out pledge cards and use spiritual gift inventories at these gatherings and recruit them for participation in these ministries
   - follow up those who do not attend with mail or personal drop-offs of commitment cards (use different letters for different segments of congregation)
   - follow up those with telephone calls if cards do not come in

7. Send the same letter to all with a pledge card and time/talent sheet. Follow up via phone to those who do not bring or send them in. Offer to bring another card or to pick up completed cards. Follow up two to three times if cards do not come in. Finally, say "I don't know what you give, but would you like me to instruct the financial secretary to put you down for the same amount you gave this year?" (Most will say "yes.")

8. Send out same letter to all with pledge card (no time/talent sheet) and take only that what comes in. No follow-up. No mention of money or giving in worship services. This is the least effective strategy—only one step above doing nothing. It will keep the "conspiracy of silence" about money in the church going and it will kill the church.

Relationship of Spiritual Gifts to Corresponding Ministries in the Church

THIS SECTION LISTS EIGHTEEN God-given spiritual gifts named in the Bible and characteristics of the person who exhibits each gift. Following each description, the corresponding ministries are listed for each gift and how they might be implemented. The first ministry listed corresponds the most directly with the biblical spiritual gift.

APOSTLESHIP

Characteristics
> Sent out to speak for Jesus, to share the good news and win people for Christ

Ministries
- evangelism
- worship/spiritual growth
- Christian witness in society
- mission in community/world

PROPHECY

Characteristics
> From knowing the past, is able to see trends in the future and fore-tell immediate future; discerns God's actions in the present and calls us to join God in these actions

Ministries
- Christian witness in society
- Worship/spiritual growth

- Christian education
- Mission in community/world
- Long-range planning

EVANGELISM

Characteristics
Bubbles enthusiastically about the good news to the unchurched about life in Christ Jesus and his church
Ministries
- Evangelism
- All ministries of the church need an evangelistic thrust

PASTORING

Characteristics
Shepherds and cares for the flock
Ministries
- Congregational (Pastoral) Care
- hospital/nursing home calling
- Stephen's Ministry
- support groups
- transportation corps
- cards, flowers, meals

TEACHING

Characteristics
Able to clarify, make meaningful the truths of Jesus Christ
Ministries
- Christian education for all ages
- worship/spiritual growth
- Christian witness in society
- evangelism
- stewardship

ENCOURAGEMENT/EXHORTATION

Characteristics
Builds others up, challenges, enables others to be their best, comforts, consoles, and counsels

Ministries
- pastoral/congregational care
- Christian education
- worship/spiritual growth
- stewardship

KNOWLEDGE

Characteristics
Is able to perceive and understand God's will and ways
Ministries
- Christian education
- worship/spiritual growth
- Christian witness in society
- stewardship

WISDOM

Characteristics
Uses knowledge in right ways, at right times, has good judgment
Ministries
- pastoral/congregational care
- Christian witness in society

HELPING/ASSISTING

Characteristics
Aids, supports those in need
Ministries
- mission in community/world
- pastoral/congregational care

GIVING

Characteristics
Gives eagerly, joyously of self and possessions
Ministries
- stewardship
- mission in community/world
- pastoral/congregational care

ADMINISTRATION/LEADERSHIP

Characteristics
Is a visionary, able leader of others toward God's vision; leads via being "servant"; organizes, delegates

Ministries
- church council
- long-range planning
- building and grounds

COMPASSION

Characteristics
Has genuine empathy for others in and outside the church, cares passionately for the "least of these"

Ministries
- mission in community/world
- pastoral/congregational care
- stewardship

FAITH

Characteristics
Has the "assurance of things hoped for, conviction of things not seen"; believes, trusts in God's love and goodness

Ministries
- worship/spiritual growth
- pastoral /congregational care
- Christian education
- mission to community/world
- stewardship

DISCERNMENT

Characteristics
Is able to see behind appearances to God's truth and God's way

Ministries
- spiritual growth
- Christian witness in society
- mission in community/world

- congregational care
- long-range planning

MIRACLES

Characteristics

Is able to see God's wondrous actions in the world today and announces them to others

Ministries

- pastoral/congregational care
- worship/spiritual growth
- evangelism

HEALING

Characteristics

Is an instrument of God's power to heal spiritually, emotionally, and physically; casts demons out—frees others from that which enslaves them

Ministries

- pastoral/congregational care
- spiritual growth groups
- mission to community/world

TONGUES

Characteristics

Is able to communicate God's messages to people of different perspectives, backgrounds, nations, races

Ministries

- worship/spiritual growth
- evangelism

INTERPRETATION

Characteristics

Interprets language and meaning of God's word to others, as did Philip

Ministries

- evangelism
- worship/spiritual growth

Local Church Endowment Fund Guidelines

1. Place the entire principal of the designated and undesignated gifts in the church endowment fund (unless the amount is too small) under the direction of a professional fund manager. (The UCC church might consider the United Church Foundation to function in this capacity.)

2. The investment criteria for the endowment fund are as follows:

   a. The long-term goal is to achieve a rate of return that exceeds changes in the Consumer Price Index by 3 percent.

   b. The fund shall seek to perform better than other comparable funds in "down" markets, recognizing this may affect performance in "up" markets, with a low probability of realizing a negative return in any one year.

   c. The asset allocation may range from 0 percent to 50 percent for equities, 0 percent to 75 percent for fixed income securities, and 0 percent to 100 percent for cash or cash equivalents.

   d. Equity investment should reflect a reasonable economic diversification. All bond holdings must be rated "A" or better when purchased, and at least half of any such bond holdings must be rated "AA" or better when purchased, unless specifically approved by the endowment committee.

e. Monies should be placed in socially responsible investments reflecting Christian values. (Secure a copy of the United Church of Christ or other denominational recommended investments to help with this.)

3. The principal of this endowment fund cannot be used without the specific approval of the congregation.

4. The income of the endowment fund that will have been earned in and by December 31 of the prior year may be used as follows:

   a. The income from gifts given for designated purposes shall be used as the donor stipulated.

   b. The income from undesignated gifts may be used as the congregation decides, including, but not limited to

   - begin a new ministry
   - strengthen a ministry of the church
   - add a staff member
   - keep from cutting a staff member when funds are low
   - give more to mission beyond the local church
   - provide a major capital improvement (roof, boiler, etc.)
   - enable building/remodeling projects
   - borrow from the principal at lower interest rates and repay interest to the principal
   - provide low-interest loans (2 percent) to your full-time, ordained pastors for the down payment on a home in your community.

   c. Should earnings in a given year exceed the Consumer Price Index by more than 3 percent, consideration should be given to the congregation to returning the excess to the principal as a partial hedge against inflation. However, a guiding principle should be that "A church is not a bank whose primary purpose is to make as much money as it can, but a church is a church whose primary purpose is to do as much ministry as it can in each year of its existence."

The best and fastest way to increase the principal of a church's endowment fund is to secure more gifts with an organized program of soliciting "continuing ministry gifts" from members.

5. Ministry boards, church staff, or members of the congregation may suggest possible use for the earned income provided in 4b above. It is expected that most projects will be identified through the normal budget development process and that all projects to be funded will require approval of the congregation at its annual meeting.

6. A thorough and complete written report reflecting income, expenditures, and fund balance is to be made available at the annual meeting of the congregation.

Appendix 9

Developing/Enhancing Endowment Funds In Local Churches

THIS APPENDIX INCLUDES SIX IDEAS for developing a continuing ministry gifts ministry (endowment fund) for your church, or enhancing an already existing one.

Ministry Visitations

Actual person-to-person visitation is the most effective strategy for developing/enhancing the church's endowment fund. The pastor and a lay person who understand planned giving possibilities will be sure to visit members of the church seventy years of age and older to talk about "continuing their ministry" in their church even after they die by making a provision in their estate for the church. They should make one to two calls per month (amounting to about one to two hours of time per month).

This kind of giving allows these older members to

- Continue a ministry in which they were significantly invested during their lifetime
- Continue being a pillar of the church throughout the future
- Continue to tithe after death even as before
- Enable their beloved church to continue its many significant ministries into the next century.

Foundation/Endowment Club and Annual Foundation/Endowment Sunday

Ask members to tell you if they have made a provision for the church in their wills or have arranged planned annuity gifts

Annually plan a Foundation/Endowment Sunday. The theme of worship would be stewardship of our accumulated assets. A bulletin insert would:

- list the names of persons who have made provision for the church in their estates and celebrate their continuing ministry

- share the purposes, possibilities, and amount of the endowment fund

- invite others in the congregation to join this Foundation/ Endowment Club

In addition, hold a special luncheon for club members to express gratitude for their continuing ministry gifts. This luncheon would also be mentioned or announced in the bulletin insert on Foundation/Endowmnet Sunday.

Encourage foundation members to invite others to join the foundation.

Perpetual Membership

Offer perpetual membership in your church to 1) those who have made provisions for the church in their estates, and (2) those who make significant gifts to the endowment fund, for example, five thousand dollars. Engrave their names on small bronze plaques attached to a large walnut board on the wall in the front narthex or another prominent place.

Planned Investment Gifts

Alert members to investment advantages through planned gifts such as

- life income gifts
- tax deduction on invested principal (approximately 40 percent)
- increased annual interest rate for life income (8.5 percent versus 3.5percent)
- tax deduction on interest income

There are many possibilities to fit individual situations. Contact the UCC Planned Giving Office or other denominational offices for more information. Depending on how a plan is set up, the church receives the principal and/or interest upon the death of the member who has established the plan.

Seek New Gifts Rather than Use Endowment Principal

Increase the endowment principal through seeking additional gifts rather than tapping into the endowment income. The mission of the church is to do as much ministry as possible each year with the income from the investments, *not* to use the income to increase the principal! The principal grows much faster and more ministry is accomplished when additional endowment gifts are sought and received.

Develop a Creative Brochure

Develop a brochure explaining the endowment fund, its purpose, and how people can contribute. This brochure should

- tell the story clearly and simply
- suggest specific ways for people to participate
- ask folks to consider making a provision for the church in their estate or to make a planned gift (life income, insurance, etc.) with the church as the beneficiary.

Notes

CHAPTER 1

1. empty tomb, inc., 301 North 4th Street, Champaign, IL, 61820, 217-356-2262.

CHAPTER 8

1. Bill Easum, from his articles in "Net Results: New Ideas for Vital Ministries," 5001 Avenue N, Lubbock, TX 79412-2993. I have found this to be the most helpful periodical regarding church revitalization.
2. Bill Hybels and Mark Mittelberg, *Becoming a Contagious Christian* (Grand Rapids, Mich.: Zondervan, 1994).
3. Bill Easum, Easum, Bandy, and Associates, 1126 Whispering Sands, Port Arkansas, TX 78373. I was privileged to spend five days with Bill Easum at a denominational judicatory staff gathering and owe much of my thinking regarding contemporary worship to him, especially in regard to the need to communicate with the younger generations using their language, music, and technology.

CHAPTER 9

1. empty tomb, inc., 301 North 4th Street, Champaign, IL, 61820, 217-356-2262.

CHAPTER 10

1. Donald W. Hinze, *To Give and Give Again: A Christian Imperative for Generosity.* (Cleveland: Pilgrim Press, 1990).
2. The Union Church of Hinsdale, 137 S. Garfield Street, Hinsdale, Illinois 60521.

CHAPTER 11

1. The Workshop Rotation style of children's Christian education is based on Howard Gardner's work using multidimensional learning that maintains that people, including children, have eight different forms of intelligences and therefore learn best when able to use their predominate form of intelligence. They are: verbal-linguistic, mathematical-logical, visual-social, bodily-kinesthetic, musical, materialistic, intrapersonal, and interpersonal. The Workshop Rotation Style develops workshops that seek to communicate the Christian faith with children by using the different forms of intelligence, with the children rotating each week among the workshops. For more information, check out <www.rotation.org> or <www.childrensministries.org>.
2. See note 1.

CHAPTER 13

1. Reinhold Niebuhr, *The Nature and Destiny of Man* (New York: Charles Scribner & Sons, 1949).

Other books from The Pilgrim Press

THE SHAPE OF ZION
Leadership and Life in Black Churches
MICHAEL I. N. DASH AND CHRISTINE CHAPMAN
FOREWORD BY LAWRENCE H. MAMIYA

This resource is a practical and functional resource that provides a public profile of the organizational backbone of black congregations within the United Methodist Church, Presbyterian Church (U.S.A.), and historically black congregations. Research for this resource was initiated to enhance the capability of religious denominations in the use of congregational studies.

ISBN 0-8298-1491-4/paper/208 pages/$19.00

THE GENERATION DRIVEN CHURCH
Evangelizing Boomers, Busters, and Millennials
WILLIAM AND LE ETTA BENKE

The Benkes seek to revitalize the ministries of small and midsize churches by helping them to adjust to the changing culture. It also offers strategic approaches that will reorient ministries to attract younger generations and take churches with an "inward focus" (churches devoid of conversion growth because of the absence of meaningful outreach to un-churched adults who comprise the postmodernist cultures) to an "outreach focus."

ISBN 0-8298-1509-0/paper/128 pages/$13.00

BEHOLD, I DO A NEW THING
Transforming Communities of Faith
C. KIRK HADAWAY

Recent talk and thinking about congregations concentrate on declining church attendance. Author Kirk Hadaway thinks an important part of the conversation is missing—how can churches, in spite of the decline, remain engaged in the mission of transforming lives? Looking at churches in new ways and holding new expectations will allow church leadership to guide congregations in the journey where transformation and renewal is constant and embraced.

ISBN 0-8298-1430-2/paper/160 pages/$15.00

HOW TO GET ALONG WITH YOUR CHURCH
Creating Cultural Capital for Doing Ministry
GEORGE B. THOMPSON JR.

This resource incorporates Thompson's research and observations on pastoring a church. He finds that the pastors who are most successful in engaging their parishioners are the ones who develop "cultural capital" within their congregations, meaning that they invest themselves deeply into how their church does its work and ministries.

ISBN 0-8298-1437-X/paper/176 pages/$17.00

FUTURING YOUR CHURCH
Finding Your Vision and Making It Work
GEORGE B. THOMPSON JR.

This resource allows church leaders to explore their congregation's heritage, its current context, and its theological bearings. Dr. Thompson provides insights that enable church members to discern what God is currently calling the church to do in this time and place. It is a practical, helpful tool for futuring ministry.

ISBN 0-8298-1331-4/paper/128 pages/$14.95

THE INDISPENSABLE GUIDE FOR SMALLER CHURCHES
DAVID R. RAY

This book expands on earlier works by treating such subjects as communal theology, theories, and tools for understanding smaller churches, worship education, and finance. His vision is to lead smaller churches to the year 2030.

ISBN 0-8298-1507-4/paper/288 pages/$24.00

THE BIG SMALL CHURCH BOOK
DAVID R. RAY

Over 60 percent of churches have fewer than seventy-five people in attendance each Sunday. *The Big Small Church Book* contains information on everything from practical business matters to spiritual development. Clergy and lay leaders of big churches can learn much here as well.

ISBN 0-8298-0936-8/paper/256 pages/$15.95

LEGAL GUIDE FOR DAY-TO-DAY CHURCH MATTERS
A Handbook for Pastors and Church Members
Revised and Expanded
CYNTHIA S. MAZUR AND RONALD K. BULLIS

Will "agreements not to sue" signed by parents or guardians protect religious organizations from being sued? These and other important questions are answered by the authors, who are both clergy and attorneys. This book belongs on every pastor's desk because the church is not exempt from the growing number of lawsuits filed each year.

ISBN 0-8298—0990-2/paper/160 pages/$10.00

THE MARK OF ZION
Congregational Life in Black Churches
STEPHEN C. RASOR AND MICHAEL I.N. DASH
FOREWORD BY CARL S. DUDLEY

The companion book to *The Shape of Zion: Leadership and Life in Black Churches*, this new book is the only Gallup supported national sample of black religiosity. Rasor and Dash propose that the black experience in America offers a significant presence in the religious landscape of contemporary American society. To illustrate their thesis, the authors provide a profile of black churches that looks at congregants, black congregational identity, liturgy and worship, congregational activities and ministries, congregational assets, and resources and leadership in congregations.

ISBN 0-8298-1576-7/144 pages/paper/$16.00

TREASURES IN CLAY JARS
New Ways to Understand Your Church
GEORGE B. THOMPSON JR.
FOREWORD BY JAMES FOWLER

Treasures in Clay Jars is designed to provide persons in training for ministry with a paradigm-shifting framework to interpret and work effectively with the complex dynamics of local faith communities. Thompson utilizes explicit and relevant conceptual and theoretical tools from fields such as sociology, economics, and cultural anthropology to engage those who will become pastors to effectively work with 21st century congregations.

ISBN 0-8298-1566-X/224 pages/paper/$21.00

To order these or any other books from The Pilgrim Press, call
or write to:

The Pilgrim Press
700 Prospect Avenue East
Cleveland, Ohio 44115-1100

Phone orders: 800-537-3394 • Fax orders: 216-736-2206
Please include shipping charges of $4.00 for the first book and $0.75
for each additional book.

Or order from our Web sites at <www.pilgrimpress.com> and
<www.unitedchurchpress.com>.

Prices subject to change without notice.